Dedication

To my beloved husband, Simon, whose unwavering faith, gentle nudges, and loving encouragement make all things possible. You continually open my eyes to life's magic.

The Hidden Magic of
Walt Disney
World

2ND EDITION

Over 600 Secrets *of the Magic Kingdom, Epcot, Disney's Hollywood Studios, and Disney's Animal Kingdom*

SUSAN VENESS

Avon, Massachusetts

Published by Adams Media, a division of F+W Media, Inc.
57 Littlefield Street, Avon, MA 02322. U.S.A.
www.adamsmedia.com

ISBN 10: 1-4405-8780-9
ISBN 13: 978-1-4405-8780-1
eISBN 10: 1-4405-8781-7
eISBN 13: 978-1-4405-8781-8

Printed in the United States of America.

10 9 8 7 6 5 4 3 2 1

This publication is designed to provide accurate and authoritative information
with regard to the subject matter covered. It is sold with the understanding that
the publisher is not engaged in rendering legal, accounting, or other professional
advice. If legal advice or other expert assistance is required, the services of a compe-
tent professional person should be sought.

— From a *Declaration of Principles* jointly adopted by a Committee of the American
Bar Association and a Committee of Publishers and Associations

Many of the designations used in this book, including but not limited to place
names and character names, are the registered trademarks of The Walt Disney Company. Where those designations appear in this book and Adams Media was aware of
the trademark status, the designations have been printed with initial capital letters.

The following are registered trademarks of The Walt Disney Company: Adventureland,
Audio-Animatronics, Disney's Animal Kingdom Park, Epcot, Fantasyland, Frontier-
land, Indiana Jones Epic Stunt Spectacular!, Magic Kingdom Park, Main Street U.S.A.,
Mickey Mouse, Tomorrowland, The Twilight Zone: Tower of Terror, Walt Disney
World. Universal Studios is a registered trademark of Universal Studios, Inc.

Cover design by Erin Dawson.
Cover images © iStockphoto.com/angelinast.
Maps by Joe Comeau.

This book is available at quantity discounts for bulk purchases.
For information, please call 1-800-289-0963.

Contents

Foreword

Magic flows out of the tricks you don't see. It is the magician's way of weaving what is right in front of your eyes with something subtle, something hidden. It is a blending of your expectation of what *should* happen with the delightful surprise of something far more creative.

Disney magic is even more elusive. Some say it's in the attractions, some say it's in the atmosphere, and some credit the can-do attitude of the Cast Members. But nearly everyone who visits the parks agrees: The magic is there; they just can't quite put their finger on where. And like the magician, Disney's magic also lies in the sleight of hand, the hidden detail.

My first visit to the Magic Kingdom was as a child. While it was great family fun and the delight in exploring a "whole new world" was already apparent, my childlike viewpoint did not see any further than that. It wasn't until my next visit in 1989 that I really understood the magic. Settled in my seat during the preshow for the Living Seas at Epcot, I was fully immersed in watching the movie about how the seas were formed and what their future might be. When the show ended, a set of doors leading to a ride vehicle, the Sea Cabs, opened with a great, satisfying *whoosh*. I was stunned! There was more to this than a film? I was also going to take a ride? Where would it go?

The answer should have been obvious, considering that the pavilion contained the world's largest aquarium. But it wasn't. The park experience was so overwhelming; it was almost impossible to do more than just allow Disney to move me from one attraction to the next, taking in only what was directly in front of me.

Those open doors with an adventure waiting beyond were a defining moment and began my fascination with Disney's flawless ability to add just a bit more.

My Disney obsession translated into yearly vacations. I quickly became an online Disney travel specialist, ultimately becoming a full-time researcher, professional travel writer, and guidebook coauthor, specializing in Orlando and Walt Disney World.

Ongoing research for the guidebook and other writing deepened my knowledge of (and love for) the parks. The more familiar I became with them, the more I began to look around for the smaller details, and the more I looked around, the more I realized how often the details that seemed hidden were actually right in front of my eyes.

Often, I didn't know what I was looking at. Sometimes I knew what I was looking at, but I didn't know why it had been placed there or what it was for. Things had clearly been done for a reason, and I couldn't bear not knowing what that reason was.

Increasingly, I began to feel the real magic of the parks could be found in the details and it became a personal mission to seek them out. Some jumped right out at me (the lanterns in the window in Liberty Square were clearly a reference to Paul Revere and his midnight ride) while others, like the unexpected For Rent sign in a window, left me totally perplexed.

What started as a diversion became a passion, and I began to visit the parks at every opportunity, specifically looking for their hidden gems. I no longer saw the attractions as rides, but instead as opportunities to seek out the details, thus viewing the story in a whole new way—a more complete and satisfying way.

The kernel of an idea formed, and within a short time I began writing and researching in earnest, with an eye toward creating a companion guide to the other Disney writing projects my husband, Simon, and I were already doing.

Further inspiration came in the form of my brother, Chip. As young adults, we had taken a vacation together at Walt Disney World, and although I was already a serious Disney fan, the parks held limited appeal for him. In fact, he was bored. But, in 2006, his wife expressed an interest in visiting Walt Disney World. She had never been, and they had a few days to spare.

We invited them down to our home for a visit and planned a few days at Walt Disney World. Chip was willing, but uninspired. I decided to show him the parks in a whole new light, and as we toured Epcot and Magic Kingdom, I pointed out the wonderful Imagineering jewels scattered all around. We talked about the backstories, we stopped and listened, and he opened his eyes wide.

In a thank-you e-mail, he told me it was the best time he's ever had in the parks, and that everyone should see them from that perspective. I agreed.

Whether you are a die-hard Disney fan, a casual visitor, or a guest who suspects there is more to it but aren't sure where to look, let *The Hidden Magic of Walt Disney World, 2nd Edition* be your tour guide. Allow it to slow you down long enough for the magic to catch up. It's all there—and now you know where to find it!

Introduction

Enter a Walt Disney World theme park and you have the Imagineers' promise that you will experience unforgettable stories. Each land and attraction is like a multilayered, immersive tale that transports visitors into the realm of fantasy, adventure, discovery, and magic. The key to Disney's success lies in the small details that flesh out the stories, making them utterly compelling and completely believable. But many of the details are obscure, and guests walk by them all day long without fully appreciating what they are and why they are there. *The Hidden Magic of Walt Disney World, 2nd Edition* is your guide to discovering these wonderful hidden gems.

Walt Disney began his animated movie empire in 1937 with the simple story of *Snow White and the Seven Dwarfs*, one of the fairy tales collected from all across Europe by the Brothers Grimm. The original fairy tales and folk stories the brothers collected were too dark, graphic, and gruesome for Victorian sensibilities, so they modified them to appeal to the current audience, adding obvious moral lessons while retaining a glimmer of what made each tale special. With each new edition of their collected works, they refined the fables further. When Walt Disney began telling the stories in his movies and theme parks, his animators and designers employed even greater modifications as audiences' tastes changed, adding romance, glamour, and humor. Today, many of the fairy tales chosen as the basis of Disney movies and theme park attractions bear little resemblance to their origins, with just a nod in the direction of the original tale.

Over the decades, advancements in technology provided new ways for Disney Imagineers to tell their stories. From the simple singing birds of the Enchanted Tiki Room to stories of adventure in Pirates of the Caribbean and the Haunted Mansion, to character-driven stories such as Toy Story Midway Mania! and *Festival of the Lion King*, the means by which the story was told grew slicker and more immersive. But one thing remains constant: No detail is spared if it enhances the experience.

And that's where the hidden magic comes in. References to world history and Disney history abound in the parks. Jokes and humorous twists on familiar subjects are everywhere. Even nods to the Imagineers who designed each park and attraction can be found throughout their creations.

Some attractions, such as Expedition Everest—Legend of the Forbidden Mountain at Disney's Animal Kingdom, Star Tours at Disney's Hollywood Studios, and Big Thunder Mountain Railroad at Magic Kingdom, are heavily detailed. Others, like Swiss Family Treehouse at Magic Kingdom, have very few hidden elements. Some attractions may not change at all over the years while others receive little face-lifts or major refurbishments on a semi-regular basis. Hence, more attention is paid to certain attractions in this book, while others retain the charm of the original hidden magic laid out in the first edition of the book.

The Hidden Magic of Walt Disney World showed how great the interest is in the small details and the story behind the attractions, and this second edition delves even deeper into these magical gems. A major Fantasyland and Storybook Circus expansion, completed in 2014, opened up a whole new world of hidden magic to explore. In fact,

Storybook Circus is practically a catalog of Disney history and Imagineer tributes.

As you tour the parks and attractions you'll find each of the hidden details listed in the book in the order in which you'll encounter them, with specific details highlighted in bold to make it easier to find them at a glance. Bear in mind, the parks are ever-changing, so if you come across a detail in the book that has been removed or isn't working, simply move on to the next thing. And remember, some attractions are dark, so pass the time in the queue by refreshing your memory on what you'll look for once you're inside.

Let *The Hidden Magic of Walt Disney World, 2nd Edition* act as a friendly tour guide, opening your eyes to the backstories, the hidden elements, and the wonderful world that Walt Disney and his Imagineers created.

And now, let's begin the journey where the World began . . . Disney's Magic Kingdom.

Magic Kingdom

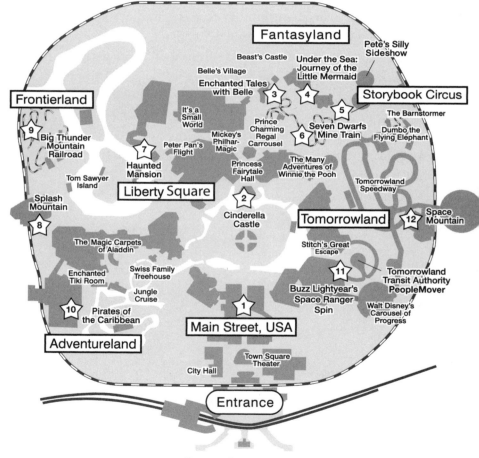

Fantasyland

Pete's Silly Sideshow

Beast's Castle

Under the Sea: Journey of the Little Mermaid

Belle's Village

Enchanted Tales with Belle

Frontierland

It's a Small World

Prince Charming Regal Carrousel

Storybook Circus

The Barnstormer

9 Big Thunder Mountain Railroad

Peter Pan's Flight

Mickey's Philhar-Magic

Seven Dwarfs Mine Train

Dumbo the Flying Elephant

7 Haunted Mansion

Princess Fairytale Hall

The Many Adventures of Winnie the Pooh

Tomorrowland Speedway

Tom Sawyer Island

Liberty Square

Splash Mountain

2 Cinderella Castle

Tomorrowland

12 Space Mountain

8

The Magic Carpets of Aladdin

Stitch's Great Escape

Swiss Family Treehouse

11 Tomorrowland Transit Authority PeopleMover

Enchanted Tiki Room

Jungle Cruise

Buzz Lightyear's Space Ranger Spin

Walt Disney's Carousel of Progress

10 Pirates of the Caribbean

1

Main Street, USA

Adventureland

Town Square Theater

City Hall

Entrance

Seven Seas Lagoon

1. **Main Street, U.S.A.:** Sit down on the bench with Goofy, located in front of Tony's Town Square Restaurant, and he may engage you in conversation.

2. **Cinderella Castle:** The lower half of the castle is designed like a medieval fortress while the top is much more delicate and fairy-tale-like, as would be common for a Renaissance palace.

3. **Enchanted Tales with Belle:** There is a wood carving of Belle dancing with the Beast in his workshop, which Maurice used as a model for the music box featured in the Be Our Guest Restaurant.

4. **Under the Sea: Journey of the Little Mermaid:** There is a memorial to the *Nautilus* from *20,000 Leagues under the Sea* that once made its home on the land that now houses the Little Mermaid's grotto.

5. **Storybook Circus:** The posters throughout Storybook Circus are filled with references to Disney Imagineers, Disney attractions, and Disney animated short films.

6. **Seven Dwarfs Mine Train:** The two vultures perched at the top of the mine's first lift hill once made their home in the former Snow White's Scary Adventures attraction.

7. **Haunted Mansion:** The new story of the Haunted Mansion's ghostly bride is based on the portrait in the stretch room of the woman holding a rose while sitting on her husband George's headstone.

8. **Splash Mountain:** Many of the animals you see on your journey are inspired by the America Sings attraction, which replaced Carousel of Progress in Disneyland when the attraction was moved to Orlando.

9. **Big Thunder Mountain Railroad:** One of the mine shafts on the Big Thunder Mountain complex diagram is Shaft #71, remembering the opening year of Magic Kingdom.

10. **Pirates of the Caribbean:** Just before you enter Castillo del Morro, take a look at the large rock on the ground to the left. Most people pass by it never noticing it looks exactly like a skull.

11. **Buzz Lightyear's Space Ranger Spin:** When you enter the queue, look at the second painting on the wall to your right. There is a planet called Pollos Prime, shaped like Mickey Mouse's profile, in the location of Orlando, Florida.

12. **Space Mountain:** The front of the spaceship suspended above the coaster's first lift hill has the markings H-NCH 1975, a reference to Disney Legend John Hench, designer of the original Space Mountain, and to the year Spaceship Earth opened.

Chapter 1

The Magic Kingdom

Touring Disney's Magic Kingdom is like taking a world journey. The park has a distinct flow, from the Small Town America of Walt Disney's childhood memory, to Europe, the New World, the American West, Mexico, the Caribbean, the Middle East, into Space, and finally, to the cartoon world of Walt Disney's imagination.

But there are other ways of looking at the Magic Kingdom as well. We will explore it from three distinct perspectives—the Show, the Facts, and a historical timeline of exploration—giving a sense of the thought and detail that went into creating an all-encompassing world filled with the gentleness of fantasy and the fascination of fact.

As a fun addition to your Magic Kingdom touring, why not go on a **weathervane hunt**? There are weathervanes on many of Magic Kingdom's buildings, and if you have a sharp eye you'll find a rooster, a moose, a hunched-over elf-like man with a long nose, and a crocodile. Do your best to find each one, but if you have trouble their locations can be found in Solution 1 in Appendix: Solution to Hints, at the end of the book.

Main Street, U.S.A.

Every aspect of Walt Disney World focuses on the Show, which invites guests to suspend reality and become part of a fully immersive theatrical experience, but Main Street, U.S.A. also tells the Facts about the making of the Magic Kingdom more vividly than any other area of the park. These elements combine seamlessly, creating a sense of Hometown America as Walt Disney remembered it from his childhood home of Marceline, Missouri. Main Street allows guests to immediately feel a sense of familiarity and, at the same time, experience excitement and anticipation for the grand adventure that waits when we venture beyond the boundaries of home.

It all begins when you set foot on Magic Kingdom property. From the perspective of the Show, the turnstiles are like the entry to a grand theater. As you pass under the train station, you see posters representing Coming Attractions, building the excitement for what's in store. Then, walk into the theater represented by the train station's exit, breathe in the smell of fresh, hot popcorn, and enter the Show. That's when the magic really takes over.

Imagine That!

Gene Columbus began his Disney career as Manager of Magic Kingdom Entertainment & Set Shows and he knows what it takes to produce great entertainment. His keen eye for quality entertainers has given the parks that "special something" that complements the large-scale attractions. Gene took his skills to the Orlando Repertory Theatre after his time with Disney and, as Executive Director, he continues to provide opportunities for today's brightest talent. He recalls his role as Manager of Entertainment Staffing at Walt Disney World: "Casting and hiring were one of the most important tasks I had as a leader. I expected the performer to come to a performance without excuses or positioning. Sing the song like you wrote it and make me believe those are your words. I looked for people who give themselves completely to the materials. After many decades it is wonderful to see a few performers I cast many years ago still performing today. However, it was the staffing process that has and continues to bring value to the company and I have been told that is part of my legacy. Selecting people who have a passion for the product, the people, and the purpose seems simple. I was never concerned about hiring people who were better than me, and I have to say it was wonderful to report to many people that I had hired. There are so many, and each should take credit for their success. I am thrilled that I had a small part in helping them along the way."

Town Square

The best blockbuster movies take your breath away, putting you firmly on the edge of your seat from the very first scene, and Town Square achieves this in high style. Although Cinderella Castle almost pulls you down Main Street, Town Square sets the scene for the experience to come, moving you through Hometown America and out into the World of Walt Disney.

Notice the entire length of Main Street is bordered by red pavement, as if the **Red Carpet** has been rolled out for you. The Fact is, when Kodak was consulted, they determined a particular shade of red enhances guest photographs, especially in direct contrast to the green of the grass.

Imagine That!

Staying within a land or attraction's theme is important, as Ron Logan, former Executive Vice President of Walt Disney Entertainment, found out when he began his career with Disney as a musician. "The first time I met Walt Disney I was a young man, and I was part of the trumpet corps at Disneyland. To my surprise, I got written up by Walt one day. I was playing rock-and-roll music marching down Main Street, and he sent me a note calling me into his office, where he said, 'There was no rock-and-roll music in the 1920s, young man.'"

On the left of Town Square are the town's services, and **Fire Station 71** is a clever nod to 1971, the year the Magic Kingdom opened. On the right are the town's entertainment venues, including Exposition Hall and the local dining hot-spot.

Across the square you'll find Tony's Town Square Restaurant, named for the restaurant where Lady and the Tramp enjoyed their romantic spaghetti dinner, which holds two charming secrets. You will find a **tribute to Tramp's love** for his beautiful lady carved into the pavement to the left of the stairs, and if you go inside and walk to the back of the restaurant, you will find them **enjoying a quiet meal** outside the back window.

There is an **old-fashioned crank telephone** just inside the right-hand door at the Chapeau, near Tony's Town Square Restaurant, and if you pick up the receiver you'll hear two women having a conversation. There was a time when phones had a party line, meaning up to twenty homes in the neighborhood were on the same telephone line and could hear each other's conversations. How could residents tell if the call was for them? Each home had its own phone number that triggered a specific ring sequence. Stay on the line in the Chapeau long enough and you may hear a nosy neighbor butt into the conversation.

Fascinating Fact

Though the results of their labors will be appreciated and admired by millions, Imagineers are not allowed to sign their work. Instead, they sometimes place little symbols of themselves, often in the form of initials or birthdates, cleverly disguised to blend into the environment's theme. You will see many as you tour the parks.

Every good Hometown America has its central park, with benches for the townsfolk to relax and enjoy a perfect afternoon. Sit down on the **bench with Goofy**, located in front of Tony's Town Square Restaurant, and he may engage you in conversation. Goofy does like to move around, so if you don't see him in front of the restaurant, look around the square. He and his bench are likely to be there somewhere!

Roy O. Disney, Walt's brother and the real driving force behind the Magic Kingdom after Walt passed away in 1966, has his own bench in the park, seated with Minnie Mouse, honoring their supporting roles in the successes of Walt and Mickey. Roy and Minnie also tend to move around the courtyard, but they are generally found near City Hall.

While you're in the area, take a look at the plaque on the left-hand side of the landscaping just beyond the flagpole. Each of the Disney parks has a **dedication plaque** with quotations from the executive who opened the park. Here you'll see Roy O. Disney's opening day comments. Take note of the date, though. Magic Kingdom opened on October 1, 1971, but the official ceremony didn't take place until October 25, once the park was fully functional.

Musician and Disney Legend **Ron Logan**, who generously shares his thoughts in some of the Imagine That! comments, has a second-story window on Main Street, as do many of the Disney Legends, Imagineers, and key people. Ron's is located above the Emporium, to the right of the second-story bay window nearest the Harmony Barber Shop. It reads:

Main Street Music Co.

Ron Logan

Conductor

"Leading the band into a new century"

Imagine That!

Ron Logan's window reflects his contributions to the Disney experience, but there is one honor he never expected. "To me, becoming a Disney Legend came out of the blue. I didn't even know what a Disney Legend was. I still don't know who put me up for it. Being a Legend soothes all the wounds. Guys I'm Legends with were guys I sometimes fought. We're best friends now, because we went through the war; we survived the battles."

Main Street

On the windows to either side of the Emporium's front door are the words **"Osh" Popham, Proprietor**. Ossium "Osh" Popham was the postmaster in the Disney feature film *Summer Magic* starring Burl Ives and Hayley Mills. Signs inside the Emporium indicate the store was **established in 1863**, a nod to the movie's debut 100 years later.

The Emporium Gallery next to the Emporium has a sign over the front door that reads, **Established in 1901**, the year Walt Disney was born.

As you walk down Main Street, the "movie credits" roll in the **upper windows** above the shops. The window of the first shop on the right-hand side of Main Street, above Uptown Jewelers, honors the producer, Roy O. Disney, and it reads: "*If We Can Dream It—We Can Do It!* Dreamers and Doers, Roy O. Disney." Walt Disney had the dream, but Roy's financial acumen made that dream come true.

In between Roy's window at the beginning of Main Street and Walt's window at the end of Main Street are the names of the **cast and crew** who brought the Show to life. Take time to stop and read them to honor these creative men and women.

Main Street's **second-story windows** actually perform a three-part function. At their most basic, they are advertisements for the town's services and business proprietors, from mortgages to dance lessons to interior decorators and so on. As representations of rolling credits, they are the companies involved in creating the Show.

The Fact is, they are the names of the Imagineers, artists, and bogus land-purchasing companies that held instrumental roles in the creation of the Magic Kingdom. Their corresponding businesses allude to the real-life roles they played in the creation of the park. Look for **Big Top Theatrical Productions**, "Famous since '55" (developers and designers of many of the World's Fair attractions that became Disney classics); **Iwerks-Iwerks** Stereoscopic Cameras (Ub Iwerks, animation); **M.T. Lott Co.**, "A Friend in Deeds Is a

Friend Indeed" (land acquisition; say the name quickly and you'll get the joke); and **Buena Vista Magic Lantern Slides**, "Treat Your Friends to Our Special Tricks" (Yale Gracey and Wathel Rogers, special effects), among many others. You will find some of these key people in other areas of the park, and in other hidden magic.

Imagine That!

Do Disney Imagineers ever experience the attractions as guests do? Michael Roddy, Senior Show Writer, Creative Entertainment, says, "We love it when a counterpart tells a story. I can go through another team's attraction and experience it as a guest, without actually being part of the design team. And I can take someone on something I've done, such as Seven Dwarfs Mine Train, and think, 'I'm going to blow their mind!'"

A window worth noting belongs to Frank Wells, chief operating officer and president of Walt Disney Company from 1984 to 1994. Look for the window titled **Seven Summits Expeditions**, up on the third story, above the Main Street Market House. Wells's window is the highest on Main Street, in honor of his love for mountaineering. But consider this: Wells attempted to conquer the highest summit on each of the seven continents in a single year—achieving six of the seven, but having to turn back before reaching the top of Everest. Coincidentally, there are also seven (count 'em!) lands at Magic Kingdom and Mr. Wells conquered them all.

Fascinating Fact

If anyone had been doing some investigation into who was mysteriously buying up vast acreages of land in central Florida, they would have found the chairman of each of the dummy companies was a certain Mr. M. Mouse! The whole secretive operation was given the codename Project X by Walt. It was finally brought to light by a reporter from the *Orlando Sentinel* who flew to Los Angeles to interview Walt and discovered he had an intimate knowledge of all the property taxes of the Orlando area. When the story broke, the cost of land in the surrounding area skyrocketed from $180 per acre to more than $1,000 per acre. The last few acres Walt purchased cost $80,000 each.

Fire Station 71 isn't the only place that points to **Magic Kingdom's opening year**. The door to the left of Main Street Fashion and Apparel also refers to this important year in Disney history. The lettering on the door reads:

Open since '71

Magic Kingdom Casting Agency

"It Takes People to Make the Dream a Reality"

Walter Elias Disney

Founder and Director Emeritus

Walt and Roy both have windows along Main Street, but there are also a few places in Magic Kingdom where their father and grandfather are honored. On the window above the china shop along the small alley branching off the right-hand side of Main Street you'll see a tribute to their father, **Elias Disney**. The tribute to their grandfather will come later, in Liberty Square.

You can find just about anything on Main Street, U.S.A., including **singing and dancing lessons**. If you stand between the tables in the small café area near the Art Festival sign and the trellised balcony just beyond Elias Disney's window, you will hear voice lessons coming through an upper-level window across the street. Keep listening and you may also hear tap-dancing or piano lessons.

Your attention will probably be focused on the castle now that you are getting closer, but notice how all the **shop windows** along Main Street are lower than traditional architecture would place them. Walt wanted small children to be able to see inside, which would not have been possible had they been set at their correct height.

Now that you have reached the far end of Main Street, look at the upper window above the Plaza Restaurant, facing Cinderella Castle. There, you will find **Walter Elias Disney's window**, the director of the Show. His window reads: "Walter E. Disney, Graduate School of Design & Master Planning— We specialize in Imagineering." While the director's name always comes first and last in the credits, the sentimental version of this placement dictates Walt has been given an eternal view of the castle.

Below Walt's name are the names of his **master planners**—Richard Irvine, John Hench, Howard Brummitt, Marvin Davis, Fred Hope, Vic Greene, Bill Martin, and Chuck Myall—who were instrumental in designing the Magic Kingdom.

Fascinating Fact

Contrary to one of the great urban myths, Marilyn Monroe was not the inspiration for the curvy character Tinker Bell in the 1953 Disney movie, *Peter Pan*. Margaret Kerry, actor, dancer, and voice talent, was the real reference model for the fairy, although she was not listed in the movie's credits. But there was more to it than that. Margaret explains that when creating the beguiling little pixie with animator Marc Davis and codirector Gerry Geronimi, she asked them, "'Is there any way that you want me to play her? Do you want me to play her aloof? Is she funny, is she a clown? What is she?' Marc Davis told me, 'We like your personality. We just want you to be you.' So

when you see Tinker Bell, that's exactly me. I could put in almost anything I wanted to for Tinker Bell to make her come alive." She adds,
"The first thing they asked me to do was the famous scene where
I land on the looking glass. I had made up my mind I would play
Tinker Bell as if she were about twelve years old and the whole world
was her oyster. She had never seen most things that she was about
to see, and I figured that she had never seen a looking glass. Why
should she? Why would they have that in Neverland? So I played it
looking at myself, and although they put it down that she's a preen-
ing pixie, actually I played it as if she's saying, 'Oh, is that what I look
like! Oh!' All except my hips. I was very unhappy with the size of my
hips, so that's why Tinker Bell stomps off."

Walt also has a **window on the front of the train station**,
directly above the Magic Kingdom sign, before you enter
the park. It is the only window you can see from outside
the park and it honors Walt's love of trains. It reads: "Walt
Disney World Railroad Office, Keeping Dreams on Track,
Walter E. Disney, Chief Engineer." Remember to look back
as you're leaving the park to see this special remembrance.

Then, as you transition through the Hub area, step
beyond the embrace of Hometown America and enter Old
World Europe as represented by Fantasyland.

Fantasyland

Welcome to the quintessential Disney experience, the epit-
ome of all Walt dreamed of in family entertainment. Fantasyland brings the tales gathered by the Brothers Grimm to
life through the graceful charm of European castles, knights,
and ladies fair. It is the embodiment of childhood fantasy

that has been passed down from grandparent to grandchild throughout the ages.

The Show element is fairly obvious: You have entered the cinematic world of the Disney classics. A more history-based story line brings you out of Hometown America into the charm and gallantry of medieval Europe. Billowing tents, heavy brick, and hand-blown glass windows evoke a feeling of long-ago kingdoms and quaint villages created through childhood imagination.

Fascinating Fact

Each time you pass from one land to another, the landscaping, ambient sound, and architecture change subtly. For example, when transitioning from the Hub to Adventureland, the architecture and landscaping along the front of the Crystal Palace change from Victorian to more colonial style, the design elements on the bridge crossing into Adventureland become more primitive, and the landscaping takes on a more jungle-themed look. What else is special about the transition from Crystal Palace to Adventureland? It's symbolic of the British Empire spreading its influence into Africa.

As you wander Fantasyland, you may notice many attractions are housed under tent façades, giving the land the feel of a medieval fair. Although it is a bit difficult to make the mental connection between it's a small world and a medieval festival, it's obvious the columns in front of the attraction are carved into the shape of **jousting lances**. Why did the Imagineers choose a **medieval fair theme** for Fantasyland? They didn't, really. Many of the Fantasyland attraction façades were not quite finished when Disneyland opened in California in 1955, so banners and decorative tents were used to cover the unfinished parts on opening day, and the theme stuck. It was then brought to Walt Disney World in keeping with the already-popular land in Anaheim.

Imagine That!

Cindy White, Consultant Designer for Walt Disney World, talks about her work incorporating Fantasyland's theme into the Castle Forecourt shows. "The tournament-tent look is an established Disney Fantasyland motif, and it seemed like a perfect fit for *Cinderellabration*, and then *Dream Along with Mickey*, sweet character revues that place the Disney characters in so many songs and stories. The little tents were cleverly engineered to provide easy set up for the technical team but also allow for the quick changes in the show. You can see from watching the show how many Cast Members, quick changes, and props there are, all part of a production on an open stage with no wings. While we discussed many different looks for the show, such as a big gilded castle gate and a more expansive tent, the two tents provide just enough space for the quick changes and props while still making the pieces removable for storage backstage if there is another show at night. We tried several variations on the harlequin pattern before finally settling on the blue and purple to complement the castle and the existing decking. The harlequin pattern is a traditional 'storybook' medieval style, and it is very prominent in the designs of Eyvind Earle, who art directed *Sleeping Beauty*, and that movie is loaded with slender, elegant tournament tents."

Cinderella Castle

You could be forgiven for thinking Cinderella Castle looks like two castles in one. The bottom is heavy and relatively unadorned in the manner of a **medieval fortress** while the top is much more delicate and fairy-tale-like, as would be common for a **Renaissance palace**.

If you have a sharp eye, you may notice the **Disney family coat of arms** standing guard over the front and back entrances to the castle.

In the mural scene inside the breezeway, where the prince has placed the glass slipper on Cinderella's foot, you'll find two Disney Imagineers. The man standing to the far left is **John Hench**, and the man directly behind the prince is **Herbert Ryman**. Hench and Ryman were the lead designers of Cinderella Castle.

Imagine That!

Gene Columbus, former Manager of Magic Kingdom Entertainment & Set Shows, Producer, and Manager of Entertainment Staffing at Walt Disney World, shares his thoughts on the emotional attachment people form to the parks, and how precious magical memories can be. "Cinderella Castle is no doubt the single thing I always look forward to seeing. It is brilliantly designed and captures the magic of that park. My father loved the castle and his idea of a good time was to sit on the porch of the Crystal Palace and watch the families walking around with the castle as a background, and seeing the beautiful landscaping leading up to the castle. I sat with him once and he said, 'Son, I wish there had been a place like this when you were a little boy so I could take you, your sister, and brother.' For his eightieth birthday we brought him to the park for the big 25th Anniversary Celebration. In honor of twenty-five years, the castle was turned into a pink birthday cake. It didn't cross my mind, but when we arrived in the Magic Kingdom my father screamed, 'What have they done to *my* castle?' Trying to cover, I told him it was in honor of his birthday, but he simply said, 'I don't like it!' I continued to explain that it was a promotional concept and would only be that way for a year or so. He followed with, 'But this may be the last time I get to see it!' At that moment I completely understood that we staff members do not own this place, but our guests do, so we need to use great care in how we treat what they consider to be theirs. The story does go on and we recovered, but I learned a great deal from that experience and think of my dad every time I see the castle."

Next, look for **the horse with a golden ribbon around the bottom of its tail**, on Prince Charming Regal Carrousel. Although popular myth states this is Cinderella's horse, its interior placement and lack of any design elements that would make it more prominent than the rest indicate it isn't really a horse designed for a princess. But it makes a nice story.

Fascinating Fact

Forced perspective is a technique used to trick your eye into thinking something is bigger, taller, closer, or farther away than it actually is. Imagineers use this technique throughout Walt Disney World to make the most economical use of space and materials. Many of the buildings you see are built, for example, to an 80/60/40 scale, meaning the lower level is built to 80 percent normal scale, the second level to 60 percent, and the upper level to 40 percent, giving the illusion of greater height.

Princess Fairytale Hall

The sense of elegance as you walk through the queue is matched by whimsical touches that let you know there is nothing stuffy or formal about the hall. **Stained-glass windows** feature Cinderella's mouse companions, Suzy, Jaq, and Gus, and one of the birds that helped make her ball gown.

Further along, the entry hall is lined with **portraits of Cinderella's princess friends**. Take note of the portrait of Tiana; she appears with Cajun firefly Ray and a female firefly that could just be his beloved Evening Star, Evangeline.

References to Cinderella and Princess Aurora can be found in the wallpaper, with the tiny **glass slipper** representing Cinderella and the **rose** representing Aurora. The pictures on the wall depict Aurora's "homeland."

Imagine That!

Imagineer Jason Grandt was instrumental in creating a regal court for some of Walt Disney World's most popular characters, and he shares the inspiration for this pretty meet-and-greet. "The story line is that Princess Fairytale Hall is a place for Cinderella and visiting princesses to meet the subjects of Fantasyland. Because our story is that this was a gift from the king to Cinderella, a lot of the design was inspired by the film *Cinderella* and by Cinderella Castle, which is an environment that complements all our Disney princesses." Why is Cinderella's glass slipper here? She has left her slipper at Princess Fairytale Hall as a gift for the Imagineers to display.

When you enter the chamber to meet Cinderella, notice the **books on the table** in front of the window in the center of the room. The open book is the story of *Snow White and the Seven Dwarfs*, and acts as a tribute to Walt Disney's first animated feature film and the attraction Snow White's Scary Adventures that formerly made its home here.

Other books here are *The Snow Queen*, on which the movie *Frozen* is based, *Brave*, *Beauty and the Beast*, *Cinderella*, *Rapunzel*, *The Frog Prince*, and *Sleeping Beauty*, each titled in the language in which the original fairy tale was written.

The walls between Fantasyland and Fantasy Forest aren't intended to be an entryway into the forest even though they were built as part of the Fantasyland expansion. Instead, they represent an **exit from Fantasyland**, the village under the jurisdiction of Cinderella Castle. Fantasyland is inside the fortress area while Fantasy Forest is the rural area outside the castle walls. It is a subtle difference in intent that reinforces the regal importance and protective nature of the castle and its courtyard.

Fascinating Fact

In the original Grimm fairy tale "The Frog Prince," the young princess does not kiss the frog to turn him into a prince. The frog, who retrieved a little golden ball the princess lost in return for her promise that he would be her companion, is fairly demanding in his requests to eat, sleep, and play with the princess. She quickly becomes angry and viciously throws him against a wall. He then transforms into a handsome prince and at her father's command, the princess becomes his bride. Not quite as romantic as the updated version, is it?

Belle's Village

There is a great deal of symbolism throughout Belle's little village, beginning with the crest attached to the right-hand side of the stone entry arch leading to Be Our Guest Restaurant. It is the Beast's crest, but it holds special meaning. **Roses** traditionally mean hope and joy; **heraldic lions** represent bravery, strength, and valor; and the three **fleur-de-lis** stand for purity, light, and France. Look for these symbols as you wander the area, especially in and around Beast's Castle.

Although Cast Members staying in character will tell you the portrait on the back wall in Bonjour! Village Gifts is a relative of Magic Kingdom's Vice President, **Phil Holmes**, you and I know it's really him. The adage "a picture is worth a thousand words" applies here, as there are several wonderful details hidden within the portrait. Tributes to attractions and lands Holmes has been involved with include **Aladdin's lamp** from the Magic Carpets of Aladdin, a **red**

apple from Snow White's Scary Adventures, and **peanuts** from Storybook Circus, all of which sit on the table in front of him. Over his left shoulder is a **strip of wallpaper** with the pattern used in the Haunted Mansion, while a **golden statue of Donald Duck** sits on a shelf over his right shoulder. This award is given to Cast Members who have been with the Walt Disney Company for forty years. Just below Donald is a **blue book** with a spine that reads *Terre de Fantasme*, which translates to "Land of Fantasy," or "Fantasy Land." The open book on the table features a **map of Magic Kingdom**, and Phil sports a **large ring** on his right hand, another symbol of his forty years of service with Disney.

Fascinating Fact

Who is Oswald the Lucky Rabbit? Believe it or not, there was a time when Walt Disney contracted his work as an animator to Universal Pictures. In 1927, Walt and fellow animator Ub Iwerks created the mischievous, long-eared Oswald, who became a successful commodity. While seeking expanded funding for the cartoons, Walt's request was rejected and he was informed his services were no longer required if he chose not to join producer Charles Mintz's staff. To make matters worse, Walt discovered Universal retained the rights to Oswald. Mintz moved all future Oswald animation to his own company, Winkler Productions, taking several of Disney's animators with him. It was a painful loss for Walt, but one that ultimately led to the creation of Mickey Mouse. In 2006, seventy-nine years after Walt and Ub introduced the character, Walt Disney Company secured the rights to Oswald and he once again returned to his "rightful" animation studio.

In keeping with Belle's love for reading, the **open book** to the left of Phil Holmes's portrait is the story of "Beauty and the Beast" in French.

Astute guests will notice a **small door on the outside wall** at the back of Bonjour! Village Gifts, which looks like it should be something special. A door for Cinderella's mice, maybe? Nope. Wrong village, wrong time frame. So what is it? It has no real part in the story of Belle's Village, but it does hide a maintenance element in charming style.

A special tribute to Walt Disney's and animator Ub Iwerks's 1927 cartoon co-creation **Oswald the Lucky Rabbit** can be found embedded in the walkway outside Enchanted Tales with Belle. Look for a section of the pavement about 20 feet from the Enchanted Tales with Belle sign, where two cracks come together to form a sharp point. Then look for a small round stone and two elongated stones. They form Oswald's head (facing Maurice's cottage) and ears (pointing toward Seven Dwarfs Mine Train).

Enchanted Tales with Belle

As evidenced by his yard and his workshop, Maurice's philosophy is "why throw something away when you can repurpose it," making him a recycler before recycling became fashionable. **Broken wagon wheels, rusty shovels, discarded cattle yokes, and cast-off window shutters** are, apparently, the perfect items for mending a fence or for hanging pathway lighting. Even his old chimney has been salvaged long after it should have fallen down.

Once inside Maurice's cottage, mementos from Belle's childhood abound. A **portrait of Belle** as a child, sitting with her mother while reading a book, is clearly a treasured possession. Notice the shelf to the left of the portrait. The **teapot and cup** on the shelf bear a striking resemblance to characters Belle will meet when she enters the Beast's enchanted castle.

The book on a table near the fireplace is open to the story of a young maiden and Le Prince Charment. But it's not the story of Cinderella and her prince; it is *Le Songe d'une femme* (The Dream of a Woman) written by French author Remy de Gourmont. This is the book Belle reads in the Disney animated movie *Beauty and the Beast* when Gaston asks her how she can read a book with no pictures. However, as you can see in the book on the table, and in the book she holds in the movie, there is most assuredly a picture. Oops!

Fascinating Fact

In the animated movie, Belle points to a page in the book and says it's her favorite part because it's "where she meets Prince Charming." While the picture is of a prince and a maiden meeting, the text on that page indicates the maiden has already met the prince and cannot stop thinking of him. The book is a curious choice for Belle, as Remy de Gourmont's writings, including *The Dream of a Woman*, are not exactly family-friendly. Even stranger? The original publication of the story of *Beauty and the Beast* was in 1740, but *The Dream of a Woman* was not written until 1899. Double oops!

The **torn corner of Belle's book** wasn't done by a naughty tourist. Instead, it remembers the scene in the movie when Belle is sitting on the edge of a fountain reading, with a flock of sheep around her. One of the sheep takes a bite out of her book, so the book here in Maurice's cottage is post-bite.

The **growth chart** you see on the wall as you proceed through Maurice's cottage indicates Belle has lived here for quite some time, since it starts at twelve months and continues until she turns eighteen. This presents a slight continuity problem with the movie, as the opening scene indicates Belle is new to the area and the villagers don't quite know what to make of her. But it's a lovely touch, and one many parents will relate to if they've charted their own children's growth on their walls at home.

Once inside Maurice's workshop, his tinkering nature becomes obvious. Above you is a light fixture made from a model Maurice designed in an attempt to invent a **flying machine**. Sketches and blueprints adorn the walls, including one for the wood chopper seen in the animated movie, and one for the recycled-cog light fixture here in his workshop.

Look at the shelf to the left of the enchanted mirror in the workshop for a **wood carving of Belle dancing with the Beast**. Maurice used this carving as a model for the music box featured in the Castle Dining Room in Be Our Guest Restaurant.

The **enchanted mirror** concept is from the original version of the fairy tale, in which the Beast allows Belle to leave the castle after she becomes his prisoner, but he requires her to take a mirror and a ring with her. In the tale, the mirror in her father's cottage allowed Belle to see what was happening in the castle while she was away, and the ring brought her directly back to the castle when her allotted time was up.

Imagine That!

Visitors can't help but stare in awe at the immense creativity that has been put into the attractions, but what sparks that moment of fanciful delight for those directly involved in the parks? Gene Columbus says, "The most intriguing thing of all is when I am hosting a friend or family member in a park and they ask me, 'How did they do that?' It's really fun, and my answer most of the time is, 'With Disney magic!'"

Beast's Castle

The architecture of Beast's Castle sets the time frame for this part of the story during the period when the prince was a beast, and had been for many years. Parts of the castle are crumbling, the faces on the architectural emblems are that of the Beast, and the West Wing clearly shows his rage and frustration. But there are two more time frames here as well. **Stained-glass windows** show the period after Belle has professed her love and the Beast has transformed into a prince again, and the **music box** in the Castle Dining Room, a gift to the couple from Maurice, hints at their future by recalling the night when their feelings—and their fates— changed.

Every guest has their own idea of which room in Be Our Guest is their favorite, but no matter which one you dine in, be sure to visit the West Wing, where the **portrait of the handsome prince** transforms into a portrait of the Beast. The Beast is clearly upset about this reminder of his former life, and he has slashed the portrait with his claws.

Another indicator of the time frame is the **enchanted rose** under a bell glass in the West Wing. If you watch for a while you'll see a petal fall off, and at the same time the prince's portrait will change to the face of the Beast. Time is running out, but as the stained-glass windows at the front of the castle remind us, there will be a happy ending.

Some of the **cherubs** on the ceiling have the faces of Imagineers as children, or the faces of their own children. They are lovely Imagineer signatures, don't you think?

Whether you dine in the Ballroom or not, be sure to take a few moments to look out the windows. Just as it did on that fateful night when Belle and the Beast danced here, a soft **snowfall** outside adds to the romantic atmosphere.

Imagine That!

Cindy White, Consultant Designer for Walt Disney World, talks about designing props for flexibility as well as authenticity: "The *Cinderella-bration* staging and arches that are now used for *Dream Along with Mickey* were a modification of the stage show I designed for Tokyo Disneyland's *Cinderellabration* two years earlier, with the gilded gothic arches at Magic Kingdom being a nice scenic addition that would give Walt Disney World Entertainment the opportunity to use them for other show projects. They are gothic in style, despite being a little squatty—due to sightlines—to be called spot-on gothic. They go with the front and back entranceways of the castle, which are covered with lovely little touches of gothic, from the light poles to the trefoils in the guardrails."

Gaston's Tavern

You can't miss the **fountain** in the middle of the square featuring Gaston and his sidekick LeFeu, the fool. And that's the whole point. Gaston has donated his statue to the village and while it is true that "il n'a pas de finesse" (he has no finesse), the statue does represent his personality perfectly. It leaks uncontrollably, it's a study in ego gone wild, and it promotes stepping on inferiors. Gaston is despicable, but somehow you can't help but smile when you see his tribute to the person he loves best.

It is certainly true that Gaston uses antlers in all of his decorating, and while he may not be the most creative of men, his use of a **barrel with antlers stuck in it** instead of an animal's head is at least more politically correct than using the real thing.

Walk into Gaston's Tavern and you've entered a manly man's world. All sorts of macho sports go on here, including a few things that are rather worrisome. Take a look at the decorative beam to the right of the central light fixture in the counter service area. There is a **knife embedded deep in the wood**. One wonders how it got there!

Every good pub has its darts game, and Gaston's is no different. Judging by the **score on the chalkboard**, there can be only one winner here. Then again, if the **darts sticking out of the walls** are anything to go by, perhaps Gaston has very little competition.

Just to the left of the fireplace in the right-hand dining room you'll find yet another set of antlers. Look closely and you'll see Gaston has left **the keys to the tavern** hanging from one of the antler's tines.

Walk around to the right-hand side of Gaston's Tavern and you'll see **L'Équipement de Chasse** painted on the wall. It translates to "The Hunting Equipment." Turn around and look at the left-hand wall of the Bonjour! Village Gifts shop. A gentler message can be found there in the words **Fleuriste Cueillez vos Fleurs**, meaning "Florist, Pick Your Flowers."

Pay attention to the subtle changes as you walk around the mountain where the Seven Dwarfs are mining. The front of the mountain has the same **forested feel** as Maurice's cottage, but the back of the mountain transitions to an "under the sea" theme appropriate to *The Little Mermaid*, with **clamshells** holding the downspouts to the walls and **fish holding up the roof** of the Cartography shop.

The proprietor of the Cartography shop, **H. Goff**, is a tribute to Disney Imagineer Harper Goff. Why was he singled out for honor here? Because he designed the *Nautilus* submarine for the movie version of Jules Verne's classic tale, *20,000 Leagues under the Sea*. Goff's design was subsequently used in the attraction of the same name, which once occupied the land that was taken over by the Fantasyland expansion.

At the top of the Cartographer's shop is a second tribute to Harper Goff and the attraction that made its home here from 1971 through 1994. The **weathervane** is in the shape of a squid, recalling the memorable scene in the movie *20,000 Leagues under the Sea*, when the *Nautilus* is attacked by a giant squid.

Inside the Cartographer's shop is another nautical tribute, this time to the **Disney Cruise Line** fleet. The map on the back wall has a *Little Mermaid* theme, but notice the names of the ships: the *Wonder*, the *Dream*, the *Magic*, and the *Fantasy*. Some of the ports where the Disney ships sail are also highlighted on the map.

There are three more hidden gems on the map, taken from scrawled notes on old sea-farers' maps. The terms **"Here be dragons"** and **"Here be monsters"** were used to indicate uncharted territory. The warning **"Beware the Siren's Song"** was a reminder to mariners not to be lured by sirens—the mythical creatures of the sea that appeared as beautiful women with hypnotizing voices, luring sailors to their death.

Under the Sea: Journey of the Little Mermaid

You'll find another memorial to the **Nautilus from 20,000 Leagues under the Sea** in the queue for Journey of the Little Mermaid, and this one is a doozy! Just before you reach the water fountains at the entryway into the indoor part of the queue, you'll see ropes wrapped around the railing. Stand on the left side of the ropes, where the wooden beam is broken, and look at the rockwork on the other side of the water. Near the waterline you'll see a carving that doesn't look entirely natural. It's the *Nautilus*, with the front of the submarine pointing to the left. You can also spot it by looking for two vertical cracks in the rockwork that point directly to the top of the sub.

The portion of the queue that extends to a vaulted area under Prince Eric's castle is only used during busier seasons, but if it is open during your visit pause near the stairway with baskets of bread, barrels of drink, and various kitchen utensils. The doorway leads to the castle's kitchen, and you may just hear the **chef frying up fish**.

Shortly after you board, your clamshell will plunge into the sea for your journey with the Little Mermaid. Each clamshell turns backward, and you can see the **bubbles** your "splash" makes reflected on other riders' clamshells, and you'll see the ocean closing over you when you look up. This same bubble effect is triggered when you return to land just after Ariel takes human form and her voice returns.

Ariel didn't know her eventual fate as she sang about wanting to "be where the people are," but a foreshadowing of her destiny in the form of a **statue of Prince Eric** sits just beyond her on the right-hand side of her grotto.

After you exit the attraction, look to the right at the two rocks on the left side of the water (ignore the rock closest to the fence). There is a hidden Mickey as the character **Steamboat Willie** here, but it's going to take some doing to see it. First, stand back a bit and look at the rock in front of you. You can see a faint outline of Mickey's left foot and leg, with the beginnings of his shorts, and a button. Now look at the rock behind it, which juts out to the right. Mickey's right foot, leg, and his shorts with the other button will become obvious. Above the shorts, his left arm extends to the rock on the far left. The top of the rock above his arm creates an optical illusion, and while Mickey's left ear (just above his shoulder) is easy to make out, his head looks a bit squashed. But stick with it, and you should be able to make out his face. Just above his left ear you'll see a rock that stands up a bit. That's his hat. Allow your eye to retrace its path and you should see the entire Steamboat Willie.

To keep within the flow of each land, we will pass by Seven Dwarfs Mine Train for now, returning here after our visit to Storybook Circus.

Storybook Circus

When this small bit of real estate just off of Tomorrowland opened in 1988 in honor of Mickey's sixtieth birthday, it was appropriately called Mickey's Birthdayland. In 1990 it was renamed Mickey's Starland, which lasted less than a year before it became Mickey's Toyland. The area reopened as Mickey's Toontown Fair in 1996, a name it held for fifteen years. During the big Fantasyland expansion that began in 2011, Storybook Circus was added as a subsection of Fantasyland, with distinct entryways through Fantasyland and Tomorrowland, and its own personality.

Storybook Circus takes its inspiration from the animated film *Dumbo*, with a circus theme that lends itself to whimsical reimaginings of beloved Disney characters. While it remains primarily children's territory, it is the perfect showcase for some of the lesser known Disney characters who blazed the cartoon trail in Disney series such as the How To and Pixar animated shorts, Silly Symphonies, and the animated anthology *Melody Time*. In fact there are so many references to animated shorts here it could rightly still be called Toontown.

Why leave a canvas as extensive as the pavement under your feet untouched when it can be used to help tell the story? Everywhere you look in Storybook Circus you'll see **footprints**, from monkeys and elephants to camels and bears, imprinted in the dirt. There are even **peanut shells** dropped by careless circus-goers. Where are the clean-up crew, Chip and Dale, when you need them?

Dumbo the Flying Elephant

Paintings along the base of the attraction help tell the story, but there are two worth noting. Look for the painting of the **pink elephants**, a nod toward the scene when Dumbo hallucinates after drinking a bucket of champagne. Another painting shows storks dropping **babies in diaper-shaped parachutes**. Where are they headed? To Orlando, Florida, of course!

While children are waiting for their turn to fly with Dumbo, they can enjoy the indoor playground based on the movie. The doghouse at the end of the slide holds a bit of hidden magic. There was no **dog named Sport** in the movie, but one of the Imagineers working on the attraction had a dog by that name, and gave him a lasting remembrance here.

The Barnstormer

When the circus comes to town, the posters go up! Here in Storybook Circus, posters to the right of the entry to the Barnstormer advertise Goofy's circus acts Aquamaniac, Tiger Juggling, Bear Wrasslin', and, of course, Barnstorming. **Aquamaniac** refers to the animated short *Aquamania* (1961) in which Goofy goes boating and ends up in a waterskiing race with an octopus on his head; **Tiger Juggling** is a nod toward Goofy's disastrous hunting adventure *Tiger Trouble* (1945), and **Bear Wrasslin'** is a reference to Humphrey the Bear, who appears in several Disney animated shorts, including his first appearance as a hibernating bear harassed by amateur photographer Goofy in the 1950 short *Hold That Pose*.

Goofy never juggled a tiger, but the tiger in the Tiger Juggling poster sure does look like the one he goes up against in the animated short **Tiger Trouble**.

Take note of the spelling on the poster of Goofy as the Barnstormer. Goofy may be soaring to new heights, but the spelling points toward **Soarin'** in Epcot. You'll find another reference to Epcot in the large sign Goofy has crashed through. Just under the banner on the Barnstormer billboard you'll see the words **An Acrobatic Skyleidoscope**. Skyleidoscope was the name of an "aerial spectacular" on and over Epcot's World Showcase Lagoon from 1985 to 1987, featuring ultralight seaplanes, jet skis, and various power boats.

What's up with the **monkey**? The Storybook Circus posters show Goofy with a primate friend, just as he had in the 2009 *Mickey Mouse Clubhouse* episode "Goofy's Coconutty Monkey." Coco the Monkey, from the *Mickey Mouse Clubhouse* television series, isn't Goofy's friend featured here in Storybook Circus, but let's just say the monkey here is a cousin of Coco, who is important for being the first Disney character with diabetes.

Look carefully at the **lowest airplane's propeller** on the large Barnstormer billboard Goofy has crashed through. The light area in the middle of the dark prop engine is a hidden Mickey.

Pay attention to the white seagulls at the upper right-hand corner of the sign, too. They certainly put long-time visitors in mind of the logo for the attraction **If You Had Wings**, which made its home in Magic Kingdom until 1987 when its sponsor, the now-defunct Eastern Airlines, faced financial hardship and declined to renew its contract.

This is the sort of hidden magic I adore. Just after you enter the queue for Barnstormer, turn around and look at the back of the attraction's sign. It looks pretty chopped up, doesn't it? That's because it was once the original sign for **Wiseacre Farm** when Storybook Circus was still Mickey's Toontown. Clever, isn't it?

The name **Dolores** can be found on the poster of Goofy as the Reckless Rocketeer as you're going through the queue, and on the crashed rocket just beyond the poster. Dolores is the reluctant circus elephant Goofy is tasked with washing in the 1948 animated short *The Big Wash*. She also appears in the 1953 animated short *Working for Peanuts*, featuring zookeeper Donald Duck and peanut-stealing chipmunks Chip and Dale. Curiously, Walt Disney had a secretary named Dolores Voght. Coincidence? Maybe.

The **skis in a barrel** to your left as you exit your plane at the Barnstormer are a nod toward Goofy's penchant for getting into trouble on skis in animated shorts such as *The Art of Skiing*, in which he debuted his trademark yell, and which led to the popular How To shorts. The life-saving ring buoy behind the skis also has an interesting name. "Yah-Hah-Buoy" sure sounds a lot like Goofy's yell.

A giant green bottle of **airsickness pills** can be found sitting in front of the Second Aid crate on your right-hand side after you disembark your plane at the Barnstormer. On the label is a picture of stylized captains' wings with a circle in the center that contains a star. Former If You Had Wings attraction sponsor, Eastern Airlines, used Big E Captain Wings badges from 1927 to 1991, which bear a striking resemblance. But the real gem here is the brand name of the airsick pills. They are **How to Fly** brand, recalling the title of the book Mickey Mouse reads in the 1928 black-and-white animated short *Plane Crazy*. In its testing phase, the cartoon did not garner the attention *Steamboat Willie* enjoyed when it was released later that year, but *Plane Crazy* was, in fact, Mickey's debut cartoon.

The green gas can to the left of the airsickness pills is yet another reference to a Disney animated short. The sticker on the front indicates it is fuel supplied by **Pedro Empresa Gasolina**, referencing the character Pedro, the brave little airplane in the animated short that bears his name. *Pedro* is part of the compilation *Saludos Amigos*, which came from the good-will tour Walt Disney and a handful of his animators made to South America in 1941. José Carioca, Donald Duck's parrot friend in Gran Fiesta Tour at Mexico in Epcot, also made his debut in *Saludos Amigos* in the short *Aquarela do Brasil*. The two went on to costar with rooster Panchito Pistoles in the animated movie *The Three Caballeros*.

Big Top Souvenirs

It's a gift shop, not an attraction, but go inside anyway as there is a bit of hidden magic here, starting with the **circus car** display stands lining the tent. Notice a Lambert the Lion painting behind the one reserved for lions, recalling the cartoon *Lambert the Sheepish Lion*. Further along, a little humor can be found in the penguins' car; it is actually a beverage cooler.

Also notice the name Lambert, upside down, on one of the smaller display stands with a base that's shaped like a **feed bucket**. You'll find buckets for Hyacinth Hippo from the movie *Fantasia*, and Clara, the singing diva who debuted in the animated short *Orphan's Benefit*, as well as other animated-short characters. The Big Bad Wolf's bucket recalls the Silly Symphony of the same name and is the "odd man out," being the only bucket that's upright.

Note the **Firehouse Five** logos here in the tent. There is one on the wall directly inside the front door and one on the back wall near the exit for Pete's Silly Sideshow. They are a reference to the Firehouse Five Plus Two Dixieland band at Disneyland, which included Disney Legend Harper Goff and animators Frank Thomas and Ward Kimball, two of Walt Disney's famous Nine Old Men.

Watch the **acrobats' tower** in the center of the big top. Just as it would during a real circus, a spotlight occasionally passes by, giving guests a view of the performers who would normally be there (but in this case, aren't).

Carolwood Park

If you arrive at Storybook Circus by train (or if you're just wandering around the area), look for the hat box on the platform up the first set of stairs just after you exit the station, which reads **Ten Schillings and Sixpence Ltd**. In the original *Alice's Adventures in Wonderland* stories by Lewis Carroll, illustrator Sir John Tenniel drew the Mad Hatter with a card tucked into his hatband, which stated, "in this style 10/6," indicating the price of the hat in question. The cost? Ten shillings and sixpence.

Check out the luggage one flight of stairs up from the hatbox. The big red suitcase reads **Red's Amazing Juggling Unicycles**. It refers to the 1987 Pixar animated short *Red's Dream*, featuring a lonely red unicycle that dreams of being a circus juggler.

The Big Bad Wolf's role has also been reimagined, as evidenced by the luggage trunk that states he is a **Balloonist Extraordinaire**. Apparently he is no longer blowing down pigs' houses, and instead spends his time twisting balloons into animals to keep the kiddies happy.

The name you see inside the train station clock is **Carolwood Park**, a tribute to the one-eighth scale model railroad and steam train Walt Disney built for his backyard and named the Carolwood Pacific Railroad. There are also pictures of Walt playing with his backyard train on the wall to the far left of the stroller rental counter at the front of Magic Kingdom.

Notice how the **train tracks** that run along the left-hand side of the Barnstormer, near Carolwood Pacific Railroad, end just before they intersect with the Walt Disney World Railroad? Nice attention to detail that makes the story seem real.

You may also want to pop into the restrooms here. They are themed as a **roundhouse**, with tracks leading to the front bays. Inside, the track-like placement of the floor tiles continues the theme.

Fascinating Fact

How does Walt Disney World keep its paint looking so vibrant, with the heavy use it gets and the fading effects from the Florida sun? Paint is touched up nightly in high-use areas, and every five years throughout the parks.

Casey Jr. Splash 'n' Soak Station

As you're splashing and soaking at Casey Jr. Splash 'n' Soak, pay attention to the numbers on the back of each circus car. The elephants' car number is **71**, referencing Magic Kingdom's opening year; the monkeys' car number is **82**, honoring Epcot's opening year; Hollywood Studios' opening year of **89** is on the giraffes' car; and Disney's Animal Kingdom's opening year is remembered by the **98** car filled with camels.

The place where it all started isn't left out, though. Notice the red hot dog cart outside Pete's Silly Sideshow.

It features number **55**, a tribute to 1955, the opening year of Disneyland in Anaheim, California, where the original Dumbo attraction debuted.

A tribute to animator Ward Kimball, one of Walt Disney's Nine Old Men and the creator of the crows in the movie *Dumbo*, can be found on the red circus car the monkeys have taken over, with a painting on one side featuring **clowns brandishing fire hoses**. The clown in the middle has the distinction of the trademark round glasses Kimball wore. Why does he get special treatment here? Because he was part of the Firehouse Five, which you'll recall from Big Top Souvenirs.

Imagine That!

Kal David, real-life lounge singer and voice of the intergalactic lounge singer Sonny Eclipse in Cosmic Ray's, recalls laying down the tracks for his alter ego's performances: "We recorded in Disney composer George Wilkins's home. He had a big room dedicated as a studio and it was state of the art. He had keyboard and recording gear and outboard gear in one large room, but no vocal or overdub gear. Outside he had a room with a washer and dryer, where he set up a nice vocal mike, which had a very warm sound. There was no light bulb in the laundry room but just enough light to read the lyrics.

"Most of the time spent was spent laughing because we would do a little bit and then break up. It was like singing in a foggy lounge. I did three days to finish my portion, then six songs and then some snappy repartee, and then we brought in the Space Angels. One of the girls was pregnant and the three of them had to go in that little room with no light. They were crammed in there and it was hot. They did all their parts in just a day. Then it was time for me to do my schtick. I didn't have much leeway for ad libs or changes at all, although there were a couple of times I would say, 'I don't think

I would read it that way.' I was knocked out by how it came out, though. I couldn't believe it. I hope Sonny will be there forever. He is like Jiminy Cricket. Hopefully he will go on long after I have shuffled off the planet!"

Pete's Silly Sideshow

Pete's Silly Sideshow is the place to meet classic Disney characters, but even here you'll find hidden magic. In keeping with the circus theme, the characters haven't just changed into theme-appropriate costumes; they have taken on new roles. Instead of meeting Minnie Mouse, guests are introduced to poodle trainer **Minnie Magnifique**. Daisy Duck is fortune teller **Madame Daisy Fortuna**, Donald Duck plays the role of snake charmer **The Astounding Donaldo**, and Goofy becomes the hapless stunt performer, **The Great Goofini**.

There are several large posters near Pete's Silly Sideshow featuring characters that don't hold quite the same status as some of the better-known personalities but still have their own fan following. **Lambert the Lion's** sole credit is for the short *Lambert the Sheepish Lion*; **Salty the Seal** only appeared in two animated shorts, *Rescue Dog* and *Pluto's Seal Deal*; **Clara Cluck's** filmography covers twelve shorts; **Horace Horsecollar** stared in thirty-one shorts; **Pete,** the ringmaster here in Storybook Circus, played the role of the bad guy in nearly ninety shorts; but **Pluto** is the clear winner, having featured in well over 100 shorts and a wealth of Disney films and television shows. **Hyacinth Hippo** wasn't in a short, but who can forget her ballet performance in the animated movie *Fantasia*?

Although the bear on the **Unicycling Bear** poster is clearly Humphrey (his name is even on it), Humphrey the

Bear never rode a unicycle in a Disney short. Instead, Bongo was the unicycling circus bear in the animated anthology *Fun and Fancy Free*.

To the left of the entrance to Pete's Silly Side Show is a large calliope with the words **Toot, Whistle, Plunk, Boom** at the top and **Melody Time Brass Horn Band** at the bottom. Toot, Whistle, Plunk, and Boom is from the Disney Educational Cartoon animated film *Melody Time*, a Walt Disney Animated Classics anthology, featuring seven stories set to music, including *The Legend of Johnny Appleseed* and *Pecos Bill*.

The tented area to the right of Pete's Silly Sideshow offers covered seating, and some of the props here are worth noticing. Many of the seats are **upturned buckets** for watering the circus animals and have Disney animated characters' names on them.

Trunks for the circus performers are stored here too, and some of them sure do get around, as indicated by their stickers. Two of the stickers reference pivotal dates in Disney history. The red trunk near the entry has a sticker for the **New York World's Fair in 1939**. The fair inspired Walt Disney to solidify the concept of corporate sponsorship as a means of paying for the construction of his Disneyland park. Although he did not like the idea of Mickey Mouse appearing in commercials, the fair included the Disney animated cartoon *Mickey's Surprise Party*, promoting the Nabisco Company. Also note the **Trylon and the Perisphere** on the sticker. They were the fair's icons and while each was erected separately at the fair, Epcot has combined them and made them the icon of the Universe of Energy pavilion.

A second sticker on the blue trunk at the back of the tent remembers the 1939 World's Fair in San Francisco Bay, also known as the **Golden Gate International Exposition**. Walt Disney attended, and it was here that he became intrigued by the world of miniatures after seeing a display by the famous miniatures artist Mrs. James Ward Thorne. Walt's fascination with tiny tableaus and the stories they could tell would translate to Disneyland, the large-as-life story he created in 1955.

And now, let's backtrack a bit to keep the flow of the lands.

Seven Dwarfs Mine Train

There is no doubt about it: The Seven Dwarfs' mine is incredibly scenic. Along with adding dynamic movement to Fantasyland, the highly landscaped mountain takes the area to a new level of realism.

When you enter the queue, the first thing you see is the Dwarfs' cottage. **Picks, shovels, and axes** hint at the hard work they do, but smaller details flesh out the story, too. **Weathered metal straps** hold parts of their fence together, all the wooden elements look **hand-hewn**, and the end of each **wooden beam** holding up the roof of their cottage hints at their coexistence with nature and the forest's animals. Even the texture of the mountain goes from crumbling dirt to hard-packed dirt the further you go in.

What are all those chains hanging from the gutters of the covered area of the queue at Seven Dwarfs Mine Train? They're **rain chains**, an artistic alternative to downspouts. They were invented in Japan centuries ago, and while they may be slightly outside the story here, they make a nice addition to the rustic atmosphere. Want some for your own home? Many garden shops carry them.

Imagine That!

Not all hidden magic is visual. Dave Minichiello, Director, Creative Development at Walt Disney Imagineering, points out one of the audio hidden gems in the Seven Dwarfs Mine Train attraction: "The queue has a surprise song in it, originally written for the film, called 'Music in Your Soup,' which we've recorded in instrumental version and added to our queue area. All the music in the queue area is instrumental, and we wanted to give it a feel that it was played by the Seven Dwarfs." "Music in Your Soup" was originally intended for the animated movie *Snow White and the Seven Dwarfs*, but ultimately was never used.

While playing the gem-sorting game in the interactive queue, the **bars of soap** squirt away from you if you try to touch them. They recall the scene in the movie in which Dopey is instructed to get the soap, but can't seem to hold on to it.

As you are waiting for your turn to ride, or if you're watching the mine trains passing from outside the attraction, notice how **each car is different**. During the creation process, scenic artists and Imagineers decided where the cars would have banged into things, or where normal wear-and-tear would have occurred. Some cars are newer, some are older, adding to the sense of authenticity.

The **two vultures** perched at the top of the first lift hill are a sentimental nod to the former Snow White's Scary Adventures attraction. They once made their home there, but have moved and are now keeping watch over the mine.

Shortly after your car enters the mine, take a quick look to your left for the sign that reads **Echo Canyon Canyon Canyon**. This is a humorous little addition you can't help but read as if you were actually hearing an echo.

The **cuckoo-style clock** inside the mine featuring little characters hitting an anvil with their hammers is taken directly from the animated movie *Snow White and the Seven Dwarfs*, and it signals the end of the Dwarfs' workday. In the movie and in the attraction it inspires them to sing, "Hi-ho, Hi-ho, it's home from work we go," and is the cue for your mine car to start its wild journey toward their little cottage and the end of the ride.

A second **Oswald the Lucky Rabbit** is hiding inside the mine, but he is extremely difficult to see, so you'll have to be quick. He is located just before you crest the hill after you pass Doc inside the mine. He is facing in your direction, carved into the beam on your left that runs along the ceiling, and he is situated where the beam appears to be split. Keep watching as you approach the area, and if you do manage to see him you can claim serious bragging rights for the rest of the day!

Imagine That!

As your car exits the mine you see the Seven Dwarfs' shadows against the wall, then you pass by a waterfall and cross a log bridge, just as the dwarfs did in the movie. But the design team didn't stop with images from the film. Dave Minichiello elaborates on the views Imagineers built into the outdoor portion of the ride: "Seven Dwarfs Mine Train is an attraction that has as many amazing views onboard as off. From the very beginning, we wanted to showcase sightlines so guests could see Storybook Circus and a little bit of Journey of the Little Mermaid, then we head inside the mine to see the Dwarfs. You come out and see Prince Eric's Castle, and an amazing view of Cinderella Castle. At our highest lift you see Prince Eric's Castle, Beast's Castle, and Cinderella Castle, so the views are spectacular."

Although she is obvious once you see her, many guests miss the **Old Hag** at the end of the attraction, poised to knock on the cottage door and perform her dastardly deed. While the attraction was being built, Disney remained silent on the "will she be included or won't she" issue. As sinister as the witch is, the attraction wouldn't be complete without her, would it?

The Many Adventures of Winnie the Pooh

This attraction debuted in its original form in Tokyo Disneyland as Pooh's Hunny Hunt, but the appeal is international. Children everywhere find it impossible to resist the cuddly cubby, in spite of the fact he and his forest friends took over the home that once belonged to the popular Mr. Toad.

When your ride vehicle enters Owl's house inside the attraction, turn around and look behind you. You will see a picture on the wall showing Mr. Toad from *Wind in the Willows* handing the **deed** to his house to Owl. Many WDW guests were unhappy to see Mr. Toad's Wild Ride make way for the Pooh attraction, so the Imagineers gave a nod to Toad's popularity and a subtle stamp of approval by having Toady give the deed to the current owner. The picture tends to move around a bit, so if you don't see it here, keep looking in other scenes.

Imagine That!

Inspiration comes from many places, including the target audience. Imagineer Eddie Sotto recalls, "When I was involved in Tokyo Disneyland, we wanted to create a Winnie the Pooh attraction that would be beyond anything that had ever been done. The Hunny Pot themed ride vehicles were wirelessly guided without tracks, allowing them to go backward, spin, and roam freely through the show. It was stunning, but there was still something missing. How did that relate to the story we were trying to tell? We then surveyed little kids and asked them what they would most want to do in a Winnie the Pooh attraction. The answer we got, loud and clear, was to 'bounce in the forest with Tigger.' We then spent the next several years developing a magical effect that would allow each vehicle to actually 'bounce' with Tigger."

it's a small world

Possibly the best-known attraction in Walt Disney World, it's a small world has a simple, childlike style that is a real departure from the more traditional artistic renderings used by the Imagineers. Artist Mary Blair's unique style appealed greatly to Walt Disney, as it does to young children who, in spite of the all-too-catchy tune, insist on ride after ride.

The **clock** inside the attraction goes off every fifteen minutes, with a cute little surprise. It's some consolation if you find yourself at the end of a long queue.

Imagine That!

Consultant Designer Cindy White talks about the creative process when designing Magic Kingdom's popular parades: "The energetic and insanely fun Move It! Shake It! Celebrate It! parade was created and directed by Tara Anderson, one of Walt Disney World's fabulous directors and a parade expert. I was invited to design the floats, but needed to work with the design package created by marketing for the park-wide celebration, which was all party hats, ribbons, and gift boxes. Tara's idea was to have a parade stop—a big moment when the parade pauses and a show happens—that would allow for the energetic DJ to host a huge dance party in the Hub. The big, wonky-shaped gift boxes and swoopy party hats needed to have the look of movement and energy, even while stopped on the street for eight to twelve minutes. Anytime you design parade units that are part of a stop, it helps to have the illusion and sweep of movement, hence the boxes with convex sides, swoopy hats, and flying ribbons."

Most of the whimsical figures in the attraction are based only on the Imagineer's creativity, but there are two characters that were taken from literature, specifically the book *The Ingenious Gentleman Don Quixote of La Mancha*. Just after you enter the Spain section of your journey, look to the left and you'll see **Don Quixote** and his comrade **Sancho Panza** in "small world" doll form. Quixote is in front riding a horse while Panzo is behind him on a donkey.

Fascinating Fact

It's a small world first debuted at the 1964 World's Fair in New York as a tribute to the children of the world. The attraction also brought attention to the United Nations Children's Fund (better known as UNICEF), with part of the proceeds from tickets being donated to the charity. Since that time, Disney has donated millions of dollars toward this worthy cause.

Peter Pan's Flight

Cross the walkway from it's a small world for a journey to Neverland, and remember to look around before your ship flies out the nursery window. Watch for the **building blocks** near Wendy's bed and just under the window, which spell out P Pan and Disney.

And now, exit the attraction and pass under the **transition area** to your left; this moves you from Fantasyland into Liberty Square. Each time you pass from one land to another, the sights and sounds change subtly. In keeping with the theme of the Show, you are now undergoing a scene change. The transition area is darker, symbolic of a fade-out, the music and ambient sound change, and when you emerge on the other side, you find yourself in Early America. Turn around and look at the backside of what was a Tudor home in Fantasyland. It has become the upper story of a colonial home.

Imagine That!

Consultant Designer Cindy White talks about adding historical accuracy to the park's parade floats: "The gilded pirate ship float that I designed that has been used in the Walt Disney World Christmas parade, the pirate parades, and others was built by a scenic shop in Glendale, California. When I began the design work on it I bought quite a few books on seventeenth- and eighteenth-century ship design and building, and invested in a set of ships' curves to draw the sections and plan the view with the right feel. From the shape of the hull to the detail sheets showing the carved seahorses and gold figurehead lady in front, there were easily six or seven times the normal drawings required, so I was scrambling to get it all done. Then, the sculptor at the shop in Glendale added touches of his girlfriend's face to my mermaid. I like the way she turned out. After researching pages and pages of drawings on yards, decking, sail structure, and keel I have nothing but awe for the people who designed the frigates and caravels that crossed our oceans. They were the aircraft of the day. My float only dealt with the challenges of driver vision, telescoping masts, and a prop cannon."

Liberty Square

Passing into Liberty Square, you have entered the New World. The footbridge over the river between the central Hub area and Liberty Square symbolically takes you across the ocean to the East Coast of the United States, while the transition area near Peter Pan's Flight takes you from London into colonial America. It didn't take long for the colonists to begin their westward trek, and it won't take you long to cross into Frontierland, but there is much to discover in the New World if you take the time to look.

Imagine That!

Disney's designers and artists are given the basic idea of how a new attraction or area should look, but they are allowed to be creative, too. Occasionally a designer's personal touches don't work and have to be redone, but having the freedom to express their personal style is important, and usually brings an originality to the project it might not otherwise have.

Columbia Harbour House offers more than just good food. Maps, artifacts, and nautical knickknacks adorn the walls, both on the first and second floors. Look closely and you'll notice each section is dedicated to either a **ghost ship** or a **ship lost at sea**. And, if you look out the front windows from the top floor, you'll notice it faces the Haunted Mansion. Coincidence? I think not!

Another interesting tidbit can be found on the wall to the left of the window that overlooks the Haunted Mansion. *National Geographic* magazine published a map of the **Ghost Fleets of the Outer Banks**, and a copy is framed here. It marks the location of all 500 ships lost along the U.S. coastline from Chesapeake Bay in Virginia to the Core Banks of North Carolina. On the wall directly opposite, you'll see the name of this particular room. Fans of shipwreck lore (or of the Pirates of the Caribbean movies) will know the **Flying Dutchman** to be a phantom ship that wreaked havoc on the seas, striking fear into the hearts of sailors as a foretelling of doom.

The window panes in Liberty Tree Tavern are made of **seed glass**, which harkens back to colonial times and is characterized by pinhead bubbles.

What is the meaning of the plaque on the wall at the end of the small alley to the right of Columbia Harbour House and to the left of the round turret near the door with the number 26 on it, with four hands, each grasping its neighbor's wrist? It is the symbol of the mutual insurance company that spun off from the **Union Fire Company**, founded in 1736 by Benjamin Franklin and four of his friends, also known as Ben Franklin's Bucket Brigade. At that time, only those who paid for protection could expect the fire department to show up if their house was burning down. Franklin's organization was staffed by volunteers who came to the aid of all. Those with an insurance policy would affix the four-hands symbol to their home and would receive compensation for fire damage to their property.

See the lanterns in the second-floor window of the round turret to the left of house number 26? They represent the **two lanterns** hung in Boston's Christ Church steeple in April 1776, to warn Paul Revere the British soldiers were arriving by sea.

Walk around the corner of the same building and look at the upper window on that side. The country folk may not be up, but they certainly are armed! During the Revolutionary War, the townsmen would place their **rifle in the window** to indicate they were home and ready to answer the call to arms.

The building number you see above the door at Hall of Presidents is **1787**, which reflects the time setting for the building's architecture.

The **chair in which George Washington sits** in Hall of Presidents is a replica of the one he used during the 1778 Constitutional Convention.

Abraham Lincoln's speech was assembled from six different speeches the president made during his administration.

Though it is often overlooked as just another part of the landscaping, Liberty Square Tree, the centerpiece in this area, has **thirteen lanterns** hanging from its branches; each lantern represents one of the original thirteen colonies.

Ye Olde Christmas Shoppe, just to the right of Liberty Square Tree, represents the cooperative effort of three colonial families. As you enter, you are in a **German immigrant's** shop. The middle section is owned by a **woodcarver**, and the back section belongs to a **musician**. The scent of pine and cinnamon enhances a comforting sense of Christmas, family, and home—themes important to immigrants far from their loved ones.

Now look at the upper window of the home next to the door with number 26 on the front. European immigrants brought their tradition of hanging hex signs on their homes and barns to the New World as a show of ethnic pride. The German family living above Ye Olde Christmas Shoppe goes by the name of **Kepple**, as indicated on the heart-shaped hex sign hanging outside, to the right of the front door. Is it a real name? You bet! It honors Walt Disney's paternal grandfather, Kepple Elias Disney.

Haunted Mansion

Prior to the attraction's reimagining in 2011, there was no official backstory. Now, the story of the ghostly bride, whose name is **Constance Hatchaway**, takes front and center. In the new story, the terrible temptress marries Ambrose Harper, Frank Banks, the Marquis De Doom, Reginald Caine, and finally poor George Hightower, in quick succession and with wildly successful results . . . for her.

Haunted Mansion has bats in its belfry. At least, it has one bat above its belfry. You can see it up there, disguised as a **weathervane**.

When you near the mansion's front door you have the choice of detouring through the graveyard or going straight in. For the full array of hidden magic, you'll want to take the detour.

Once inside the graveyard, take note of the first large headstone. **Grandpa Marc** refers to Marc Davis who, along with Claude Coats, was the primary designer of the Haunted Mansion. **Francis Xavier**, just a bit further on, is Francis Xavier Atencio (a.k.a. X Atencio), script writer and lyricist of the attraction's theme song, "Grim Grinning Ghosts." **The Ravenscroft tomb** in the shape of a pipe organ honors Thurl Ravenscroft, voice of the broken singing bust in the Haunted Mansion's graveyard scene. **Master Gracey's memorial** remembers Yale Gracey, creator of many of the Haunted Mansion's illusions, and finally, the tombstone with eyes that open and close honors **Madame Leota**, your séance host and former Imagineer Leota Toombs Thomas.

Fascinating Fact

Guests rarely get to see this lovely bit of hidden magic, but if you use the "chicken exit" before boarding a Doom Buggy, or if you enter through the disabled access, you'll be escorted down the "servant's hallway" where you'll see a series of valet bells with a name and location in the mansion listed under each bell. They honor Haunted Mansion Imagineers, and are listed as follows:

- Ambassador Xavier's Lounging Lodge (Francis Xavier Atencio, Haunted Mansion script writer and lyricist of "Grim Grinning Ghosts")
- Madame Leota's Boudoir (Leota Toombs Thomas, Madame Leota)
- Grandfather McKim's Resting Room (Sam McKim, artist who created the original drawings for Haunted Mansion)
- Uncle Davis's Sleeping Salon (Marc Davis, co-lead Imagineer)
- Master Gracey's Bedchamber (Yale Gracey, special effects)
- Colonel Coat's Breakfast Bearth (Claude Coats, co-lead Imagineer)
- Professor Wathel's Reposing Lounge (Wathel Rogers, Audio-Animatronics).

Prior to the reimagining, popular myth held that a sawn-off post embedded in the pavement at the end of the attraction was meant to be the bride's wedding ring. As a nod to this long-held legend, Imagineers added an **official bridal ring**, which can be seen in the pavement in the small fenced-off area just after you leave the graveyard. Look at the ground where the brick wall juts out. The right-hand corner at the bottom of the square pillar points directly to the ring.

It could be argued the long-held myth of a bridal backstory was the catalyst for change, and Disney's response is that the story is now based on one of the paintings in the stretch room. When you are asked to move to the dead center of the room and the paintings begin to stretch, notice the one of a **woman sitting on a headstone** holding a rose. She is the ghostly bride, and the ill-fated George, now resting six feet under with an axe in his skull, is just one of her victim grooms.

As you would expect, there are exactly **thirteen candles** on the cake in the ballroom scene.

When you reach the attic, listen as the bride recites passages from her **wedding vows**. They take on new meaning with the emphasis she places on them. Listen to the way she says, "as long as we both shall live," "in sickness and in wealth," and "for better or for worse." You can't help but think her groom won't live long, and that he'll have more worse than better. And you'd be right.

This is one busy bride! She's been married five times, with each **wedding date** depicted in its corresponding scene. Her first marriage occurred in **1869**, as seen on the lacy book propped up on a table in the first scene on the right-hand side; she remarried in **1872**, the date featured in the center of the banner in the second scene; and in **1874**, **1875**, and **1877** she had the dates engraved on her wedding portrait frames.

If you have a sharp eye and look quickly you may also see her flowery yellow **marriage certificates**. They are difficult to see in the dim lighting, so your best bet is to look for the certificate in the 1874 scene, on the right-hand side of the track, in a frame to the left of the trunk. If you're sitting on the left side of your Doom Buggy, look hard and you may see one in the 1872 scene, just to the left of the small three-tiered white table on the left side of the scene.

Besides the obvious creepiness of the groom's head disappearing from each wedding portrait, notice the subtle change in the **bride's disposition**. In the first portrait she is suitably circumspect. By the time she weds husband number five she can't quite contain her glee. The smirk on her face grows progressively more pronounced. By the time you reach the bride herself, just before you exit the attic for your tumble into the graveyard, she's absolutely beaming as she grasps a hatchet like it is a bouquet of flowers.

An interesting little tie-up with Pirates of the Caribbean can be found in the portrait of Constance with husband number four. Reginald is sitting in the same **elaborate chair** Captain Jack Sparrow sits in during the treasure scene at the end of the ride.

Your first encounter with the **ghostly bride** herself comes at the end of the wedding vignettes. She's holding a hatchet, and she seems pretty pleased with herself. Considering her maiden name is Hatchaway, she has chosen an interesting weapon to do away with those pesky grooms.

The caretaker in the graveyard scene certainly is frightened. Watch how his **lantern** shakes. And you might be frightened too when you realize he and his dog are the only living beings in the graveyard. What does that say about *you*, bearing in mind you just fell off the roof?

Fascinating Fact

Along with voicing one of the singing busts in the graveyard scene which belts out the mansion's theme song, "Grim Grinning Ghosts," Thurl Ravenscroft was the voice actor for Kellogg's Frosted Flakes cereal mascot Tony the Tiger, and sang "You're a Mean One Mr. Grinch" in the 1966 television special *Dr. Seuss' How the Grinch Stole Christmas*. His portfolio with Disney is vast. Listen for him when you pass the singing frogs on Splash Mountain, and also in Country Bear Jamboree, where he gives voice to the buffalo named Buff.

There certainly are a lot of ghosts at this "swinging wake," and if you look carefully as you travel through the Haunted Mansion you'll notice they have gathered from various countries and various points in time. Look for the **duelists** and a **medieval king** in the ballroom scene, and an **Egyptian mummy** sitting in a sarcophagus, a **king and his queen on a seesaw**, and a **Victorian couple** enjoying champagne in the graveyard.

The **corpulent opera singer** to the left of the crypt at the end has an interesting tie-up with Imagineer Harriet Burns. Harriet's gravestone tribute, before you enter the mansion, reads, "First lady of the opera, our haunting Harriet. Searched for a tune but never could carry it," and here in the ghostly graveyard we have a genuine "haunt" singing for all she's worth.

Finally, in keeping with the lesson in U.S. geography, once you leave Liberty Square (the East Coast), you symbolically travel with the pioneers as they make their way westward into unknown territory and you make your way into a new land.

Frontierland

As you pass into Frontierland from Liberty Square, you are symbolically crossing the Mississippi River and journeying west. The transition is gentle but obvious. Building materials in Frontierland are rough-hewn and there is a sense of excitement in the air, as if a gunfight could break out at any moment. It's the land of Davy Crockett and Buffalo Bill Cody, where anything could happen!

Tom Sawyer Island

Located in the Rivers of America, Tom Sawyer Island is a great place for a midday break. Once you reach the island, stroll down the pathway to the right of the boat dock to Harper's Mill. The gears that turn the water wheel hold an interesting little surprise for those who take the time to look. The large, horizontal gear in the middle is home to a little **bluebird** that has made her nest between the cogs. Fans of the Silly Symphony series may recognize the reference to the storm-tattered bluebird nest in the 1937 Academy Award–winning short *The Old Mill*, the first film to use the multiplane camera.

Imagine That!

Michael Roddy, Senior Show Writer/Show Director, WDW Parks and Resorts, explains the Disney ethos when it comes to creative ideas: "You never throw away anything. You always keep the scripts and the writing. There are ideas you can reuse and repurpose, and they're always valid. You can take pieces and parts that work, especially in a theme park."

The **Ambush Cave** is a fun place for youngsters to burn off excess energy, and it holds a bit of a mystery among the geodes found in its depths. Notice how the water flowing at the base of the crystal wall seems to run uphill. It may take a moment to see, but that water is definitely flowing the wrong way. Mysterious? Maybe. Look more closely and you'll notice the floor is tilted to create an optical illusion for a bit of fun.

Pay a visit to Fort Langhorn, named for Samuel Langhorne Clemens, better known as Mark Twain, the author of *The Adventures of Tom Sawyer*, near the back of the island. There are **guns** in the turrets for a little impromptu target practice. You may even get a shot at the runaway train over at Big Thunder Mountain.

While you are on the island, look across the river at the dock in front of Big Thunder Mountain Railroad. The sight-seeing tours advertised are a tribute to the long-gone **Mike Fink Keel Boats** attraction located here from 1971 until 1977.

Return to Frontierland and journey farther into the wilderness, and into American folklore. Pecos Bill was the stuff of legend in the Old West, with stories told of his superhuman feats. He was "the toughest critter west of the Alamo," digging out the Rio Grande with a stick when he needed water and shooting out all the stars in the sky, save one, which became the symbol of the Lone Star State, Texas. The **framed document** near one of the Pecos Bill Tall Tale Inn and Café exits gives an abbreviated version of the Pecos Bill story. Look a little closer and you'll find Pecos Bill's **Code of the West**, offering menfolk some good advice about what not to do in front of women and children.

The Pecos Bill Café gives a nod to the Disney animated short story and, more important, serves as a transition out of Frontierland into the Mexican end of Adventureland. Take a look at the roof of the café. Notice how the front area is pure Wild West saloon, but when you round the corner it takes a Spanish Mission–style turn, common in both California (represented by the Train Depot near Splash Mountain) and Mexico. It also blends harmoniously with the Caribbean theme as you move farther into Adventureland.

Having reached the West Coast and the train station at the terminus of the transcontinental railroad, you can't miss the two mountain ranges reaching skyward, but don't worry about them for now. Instead, head up the stairs to the train station itself, then stop and listen. You will hear Morse code emanating from the telegraph office, transmitting **Walt Disney's opening-day speech** at Disneyland in California.

Splash Mountain

Splash Mountain (whose proper name is Chick-a-Pin Hill) is based on the story in *Song of the South* as told by Uncle Remus, but it has somehow made its home in the American West. Although technically it represents the Deep South (the states of Georgia, Florida, Alabama, Louisiana, and Mississippi) and should be painted deep clay-red to represent Georgia's soil, a little creative color mixing went into blending it more harmoniously with Big Thunder Mountain, thus maintaining the theme, at least visually.

Many of the animals you see on your riverboat journey are inspired by Imagineer Marc Davis's attraction, **America Sings**, which replaced Carousel of Progress in Disneyland when the attraction was moved to Walt Disney World at the request of sponsor General Electric. Watch for **singing bullfrogs** in floppy hats, **white geese**, a **drummer porcupine**, a **raccoon** playing the harmonica, and **baby opossums** hanging over the river by their tails. The final showboat scene with singing and dancing **chickens** and a **crocodile trio** are also a tribute. Even the **pop-up gopher** and the **vultures** who gleefully bid you farewell before you hurtle into the briar patch made their debut in America Sings.

As you make each small drop, the drama and the danger increase. But there is another thread running through each changing scene, too. Splash Mountain is based on the Disney movie *Song of the South* and the gentle moral tales told by kindly Uncle Remus. When you reach the top of the attraction after the second small lift hill you have entered the "How Do You Do" segment of the movie in which Uncle Remus is going fishing, and the line "What goes up is sure to come down" is a foreshadowing of what you'll be experiencing shortly. Just after the first small drop the scene continues, blending with the story "Br'er Rabbit Runs Away" and a quick nod to "Everybody's Got a Laughing Place," which is presented again in the beehive scene after the next drop. The final scenes when Br'er Rabbit has been captured and is thrown into the briar patch are from "The Tar Baby." And finally, the attraction's theme song, "**Zip-A-Dee-Doo-Dah**," is sung by Uncle Remus, Br'er Rabbit, and Br'er Bear throughout the movie.

Drop by the Briar Patch gift shop on your way out and you'll see Br'er Rabbit's home up near the ceiling. Look carefully and you'll see a portrait of *Whistler's Mother*, rabbit-style.

Big Thunder Mountain Railroad

Big Thunder Mountain Railroad has become a true Disney classic, in part because it's a terrific coaster the whole family can enjoy and in part because of its exceptional theme. In 2012 the story of Big Thunder Mountain was reimagined, and the abandoned mountain is a working mine again. You are embarking on a tour of Big Thunder Mining Company—through the Mining Office, Explosives Magazine Room, Foreman's Post, and the Ventilation Service Room. Along the way you can blast a mine shaft, pump air into the mines, and check out the miners' progress deep beneath the ground before you set off on your own journey.

Notice the name on the Pay Rates sign, to the right of the barred window in the Mining Office. The paymaster here is **G. Willikers**.

There are two signs on the wall just after the Mining Office. Check out the name of the proprietor of the Big Thunder Mining Mountain Company Store. Apparently it is owned by a Greek man by the name of **Costas A. Lott**. Or maybe it's a nod toward the expense of Disney's reimagining of the entire queue, which tells the attraction's new story.

Crates in the rafters of the Explosives Magazine Room contain dynamite from **Western River Explosives**, and while the dynamite was contracted by **Lytum and Hyde** (an obvious warning!), the brand's origin is somewhat less obvious. It refers to Western River Expedition, a never-built boat ride once intended for Frontierland.

You will find a tribute to Imagineer Tony Baxter here too. The **portrait in the rafters** as you make your way through the explosives section is meant to be the founder of the mine, Barnabas T. Bullion, but it's really Baxter, designer of the original Big Thunder Mountain Railroad. There is a second tribute to him on the back of the Assay Report information board. Look for **T. W. Baxter** on the Automatic Train Break diagram.

The Butterfly Stage Line sign, on the right-hand wall shortly after the Assay Reports board, references **Thunder**

Mesa and **Rainbow Ridge**. Both, along with **Rainbow Mountain Stagecoach Ride**, were attractions built on the land now occupied by Big Thunder Mountain in Disneyland. **Carolwood Pacific Railroad Company**, also mentioned in the ad, refers to Walt Disney's backyard railroad setup.

The wooden name plates attached to the door of the Fusing Cage, just after you enter the Explosives Magazine Room, honor several Disney Imagineers.

- **Little Big Blaine** is a reference to sculptor Blaine Gibson
- **Matchstick Marc** honors Disney Legend Marc Davis.
- **Jolley the Kid** (Bob Jolley, Big Thunder Mountain Railroad designer)
- **Buckaroo Burke** (Pat Burke, show set designer)
- **Calamity Clem** (Clem Hall, concept artist)
- **Skittish Skip** (Skip Lange, rockwork designer)
- **Wild Wolf Joerger** (Fred Joerger, rockwork designer)
- **Mama Hutchinson** (Helena Hutchinson, figure finishing)

Just before you enter the Ventilation Service Room you'll see a diagram of the entire Big Thunder Mountain complex. Under the drawing of the highest peak you'll see the words **Rainbow Caverns**, a reference to Rainbow Caverns Mine Train, an attraction that ran through the Living Desert in Disneyland from 1956 to 1960. The mine shaft diagrammed underneath Rainbow Caverns is **Shaft #71**, remembering the opening year of Magic Kingdom.

Once inside the Ventilation Service Room, you have the chance to pump air into the mines below using the **Autocanary Air Quality Analyzers**. As you crank the handle on each one, watch the top of the big white dial. You'll see moving pictures of a bat, a cowboy, a cowboy on a horse, and a buffalo.

One of the birdcages in the Ventilation Room has the name **Rosita** on it, referencing the question "What ever happened to Rosita?" asked by José in Walt Disney's Enchanted Tiki Room. It looks like she became the canary in the coal mine. You'll see her golden cage hanging above three burlap sacks, just to the left of the Autocanary Air Quality Analyzers.

The **Hard Times Café** sign on the left side after you exit the Ventilation Room advertises apple dumplings as the specialty of the house, but in reality it is a tribute to the 1975 Disney movie *The Apple Dumpling Gang*. In the movie, there is also a mention of the Hard Times Café.

As you retrace your steps to the train station on your way into Adventureland, you have symbolically reached the West Coast, completing your cross-country trek. But lands beyond America are calling for those brave enough to face the dangers of the jungle, pirates on the high seas, and a room full of loud, singing birds.

Adventureland

With the comforts of Hometown America, the mellow charm of Europe, and the thrill of discovering the New World behind you, the next step is to head off on a grand adventure exploring Mexico, the Caribbean Islands, Polynesia, and oddly enough, the Middle East. In terms of the Show, it is the realm of *In Search of the Castaways*, *The Jungle Book*, *Swiss Family Robinson*, *Aladdin*, and the Pirates of the Caribbean movie series.

As you round the corner from Frontierland into Adventureland, the architecture is distinctly Spanish. Moving farther along, the details transition beautifully into the flavors of a Caribbean island, and then become a whole new world as you fly over the imaginary Middle Eastern realm of Agrabah before you land, somehow, in the South Seas.

Pirates of the Caribbean

Pirates of the Caribbean recalls the 1700s West Indies during the time the Spanish were finding gold in what would become the United States. Just before you enter Castillo del Morro, take a look at the large rock on the ground to your left. Most people pass by it never noticing it looks exactly like a **skull**.

Once inside the castle, there are two separate queues that wind their way toward the boarding area. In keeping with the story, the Standby queue takes you through the **soldier's living quarters** while the FastPass+ queue takes you through the **castle's dungeon**. The dungeon queue holds the hidden magic, and that's the one we'll explore.

As you walk toward the boarding area, watch for a window with bars on it, on your right-hand side. If you look into the cell below, you'll see another Imagineer signature. Disney Legend Marc Davis has marked the attraction with his love of chess. The two **skeletons playing chess** are at a total impasse. In keeping with the Imagineer's obsession with accuracy, Davis researched past masters tournaments for a no-win outcome, and the chess pieces were correctly placed on the board between the skeletons so they would appear to ponder their next move for eternity.

Once you begin your water journey, you'll come upon one of the neatest bits of visual hidden magic in the Magic Kingdom. The rock formation on your left-hand side, just as the pirate beach comes into view, looks like an **evil skull with teeth**. But wait. Keep looking at it as you pass by. It appears to be a single rock from a distance, but when you reach it you can see that it's an illusion created by four separate rocks. Ragged teeth are first, then the nose, then the right eye, then the left eye and the top of the skull.

In 2006 Jack Sparrow and Captain Barbossa from the Pirates of the Caribbean hit movie series were added, and in 2012 the **mermaids** arrived. First, you'll hear them singing "My Jolly Sailor Bold." Then, if look over the side of your boat you may see a **green, shimmering light** following you, accompanying the siren song of a mermaid attempting to lure you in. This effect isn't always working, but when it is, it's surprisingly eerie.

As you round the corner where the shipwrecked pirates' bones lay scattered on the beach, pay attention to the **skeleton in the boat**. The remains clearly show this was no pirate! Instead, the mermaid features are a nod toward the hit movie *Pirates of the Caribbean: On Stranger Tides*.

When you reach the pirate ship and war breaks out, there will be an awful lot of cannon fire going off. Why do the **cannonballs** raining down around you make an orange splash? Because they're hot when they enter the water.

Although it is difficult to see in the dark, look for the crest as you pass by the last scene, above where Jack Sparrow is laughing over his loot. Wouldn't you know it, Imagineer Marc Davis came as close to a signature as possible when he added the faintly Spanish-sounding name **Marci Daviso** to the crest. Mr. Davis didn't miss another chance to express his love of chess. He has placed **rooks** in the upper right and lower left corners of the crest.

Head across the walkway to the Tortuga Tavern (now owned by A. Smith, better known as Blackbeard's daughter Angelica) for more pirating magic. Inside the restaurant on a window ledge at the back of the room you'll find a book open to the **crew roster** for the *Black Pearl*. A certain ego-driven pirate (Jack Sparrow) has crossed out Hector Barbossa in the area reserved for the captain's name and has scrawled his own name in its place.

It's hard to say if the **bullet holes** along the stairway wall leading up to apartments in the tavern's courtyard were caused by Barbossa after seeing evidence of treachery in the book, but you can bet Jack Sparrow was involved somehow!

Before Miss Smith took over, the restaurant was called **El Pirata y el Perico**. You'll find its former sign perched on a beam near the ceiling in the outdoor dining area, just before you reach the open courtyard.

It was vital to make the most of the space available while maintaining the correct theme in each land. To that end, the Adventureland side of the walkway linking to Frontierland near the Magic Carpets of Aladdin is Polynesian in style. If you walk through the passageway, however, and look at the same walkway from the Frontierland side, it looks like a horse-and-carriage entryway.

The Jungle Cruise

Check out the list of **missing boats** in the Jungle Cruise line. It seems some of their passengers (such as Ilene Dover) are missing, too. Perhaps that's the risk you take when you traverse the Amazon, Congo, Nile, and Mekong Rivers all in one go, and since you are about to do just that, you may want to keep an eye on everyone in your group!

Once upon a time there were stickers on shipping crates (really the former FastPass machines) that referred to characters from the sorely missed **Adventurers Club** nightclub that used to make its home in Downtown Disney. But fear not! The references are not gone; they've just moved. You'll find them on tags inside the wire cage at the start of the queue.

Imagine That!

Even the most creative of Imagineers need extra insight when innovative new "stories" are introduced. Ron Rodriguez recalls, "Writer Roger Cox was a little guy with an eclectic personality. We were on the road once, talking about the Adventurers Club, and I said, 'Break down the concept, Roger. I understand individual concepts, like the Librarian, but I don't understand the overall concept.' In this big, booming voice Roger said, 'Well, Ron, let me explain this to you!' He was like an actor himself, and while he explained the whole concept, I still didn't get it. But it worked!"

Just after you pass through the Jungle Cruise turnstiles, notice there is a large, hairy, scary **tarantula** in a cage on your right-hand side. Ask the attending Cast Member about the spider. Go ahead . . . ask!

While you're waiting in line for the Jungle Cruise, look across the river. See that **small hut** that looks like it has a straw roof? With the heat, rain, and humidity in Florida, that roof wouldn't last long if it were real straw. Instead, it's made of metal strips. The ability to create a lasting thatched roof was only implemented once Disney's Animal Kingdom was under construction. Authentic thatching grass and Zulu craftsmen were brought in from KwaZulu-Natal in South

Africa to create the thatched roofs you see in the Africa section of Animal Kingdom.

As you travel the rivers, your boat will pass by the rear half of a crashed **Lockheed airplane**. The front half can be seen in the *Casablanca* scene at Disney's Hollywood Studios' Great Movie Ride, which holds another surprising secret.

Tomorrowland

After exploring the world, the next frontier to conquer is the future, specifically as it relates to space. The Show theme of Tomorrowland is firmly of the science-fiction variety, with all things metal and machinery, most of it in motion. Even the pavement puts you in mind of the planets and what's out there just beyond our reach. Things buzz around you and above you, with progress as the theme du jour.

Tomorrowland was intended to be a **working city** and the headquarters for the League of Planets. As you look around, notice all the community's needs are catered for: transportation, news, dining, shopping, and communication. Whether you're a human citizen, an alien, or a robot, everything you need is right here!

Stitch's Great Escape!

The first attraction you reach when you enter Tomorrowland from the Hub is Stitch's Great Escape!, housed in the building on your left. Many of the signs inside the attraction are written in a peculiar **alien alphabet**; however, they can be translated into English if you read carefully. In particular, look for signs reading, Galactic Federation and Prisoner Identity for easy alien-to-English comparisons.

There are seven **hidden Stitches** in the mural that spans the upper walls inside Mickey's Star Traders in Tomorrowland. From left to right, starting along the back wall, they are: (1) the front of the red train, (2) and (3) two windows on the glass buildings, (4) the satellite dish, (5) loops in road, (6) the domes (over the door), and (7) the golf-ball-style building. You can also see Stitch as himself just below the red train, and in the Merchant of Venus mural behind the cash register.

Fascinating Fact

While hunting for hidden Mickeys is a popular pastime, the mouse isn't the only character that hides in the attractions. Other characters, such as Donald Duck, Minnie Mouse, Tinker Bell, and even Baloo from *The Jungle Book* all have hidden likenesses in the parks.

Tomorrowland Speedway

Tomorrowland Speedway is fairly basic, but still has a few interesting items worth noting. Shortly after you enter the queue, there are **track maps** on the wall that are the layout of the speedway tracks at Disneyland in California, Tokyo Disneyland, Disneyland Paris, and Hong Kong Disneyland.

As your racecar zooms past the first bridge you'll see the speedway's version of the Indianapolis Speedway's **Brickyard** embedded in the track. It is a relic from the time when Tomorrowland Speedway was called Tomorrowland Indy Speedway.

While you are standing in front of Tomorrowland Speedway, stop and listen. Hear that sound? Nope, you don't, because there is no sound. You have entered the only area of the Magic Kingdom where music is not piped in. Why not?

Because there was no natural way to link Tomorrowland to Fantasyland, so the Imagineers chose not to transition guests through music.

Buzz Lightyear's Space Ranger Spin

This is the attraction most likely to make children (and competitive folks!) insist on a second or third ride so they can better their score. You'll be so busy concentrating on the targets that you aren't likely to look for hidden gems, and to be honest, this ride really is all about the end result. Even so, there are a few things to look for when you're not occupied with defeating Evil Emperor Zurg.

When you enter the queue, look at the second painting on the wall to your right. There is a planet called **Pollos Prime**, shaped like Mickey Mouse's profile, in the location of Orlando, Florida.

If you enter the area at the right time, you may hear Zurg say, **"Guards, seize them! And their little green friends, too!"** Listen for it just after you leave the first scene. It is a takeoff on the Wicked Witch of the West's comment in the movie *The Wizard of Oz*, when she tells Dorothy, "I'll get you, my pretty. And your little dog, too!"

Tomorrowland Transit Authority PeopleMover

Formerly called the WEDWay PeopleMover after Walter Elias Disney, this fan-favorite rarely has a wait. It's a pleasant ride, especially when it's hot and you can truly appreciate the breeze. The TTA passes by a model of a city, giving us a glimpse of how Walt envisioned the **City of the Future** (which eventually came into being, to some degree, as Epcot), and it is the only place you can see inside Space Mountain from the outside.

Even more remarkable, though largely unnoticed by guests, is the fact the TTA travels its entire 4,574-foot length without the benefit of any onboard moving parts. It is all driven by **magnets**.

Listen closely as you near the end of your ride on the TTA. Hear that page for "**Tom Morrow, Mr. Tom Morrow**"? Tom was the Audio-Animatronic head of Operations in the now-extinct Mission to Mars attraction.

Fascinating Fact

What is this "linear induction" that makes the TTA move? It's a process that starts with electricity in the tracks making contact with coils in the ride vehicle, which propels the vehicle forward. Shortly after leaving the boarding area, the vehicle encounters a magnetized motor that terminates the electrical connection and initiates forward motion via magnetic motors.

News travels fast in the future. Take a look at the **Tomorrowland Times** being sold by the robot near Astro Orbiter, just to the right of the entry to Tomorrowland Transit Authority. Then, walk around to the right, toward the Lunching Pad fast-food counter. See the **phone booth**? By now, you know what to do. Pick up the receiver and listen!

Walt Disney's Carousel of Progress

Serious Disney geeks know that Carousel of Progress is a groundbreaking attraction that helped set the wheels in motion for advancements in Audio-Animatronics, and indeed for the creation of the Magic Kingdom itself. Gentle and unassuming, it is often overlooked in favor of big-thrill attractions, but it's chock-full of wonderful hidden magic.

For the best chance at seeing these gems, sit in the center of the theater, or just to the right of center.

While you're enjoying the show, keep an eye out for a **cat in each scene**. See if you can find them on your own, then check Solution 2 in Appendix: Solutions to Hints.

You may notice a few incongruent elements in the story, including the **unnamed girl** in the wash-day scene, cranking the handle of the washing machine while Sarah does the ironing; a **paint mixer** being used in the Rumpus Room scene, though Sarah is wallpapering, not painting; and Grandma's comment, "**Give him a left, ya big lug!**" during a wrestling match rather than a boxing match.

There are several modern-day references to Mickey Mouse in Carousel of Progress. In the 1940s Halloween scene, look for a **Sorcerer Mickey hat** on the tuffet next to Patricia as she uses her exercise machine. We'll find a few more in the final scene, too.

When you reach the 1920s scene celebrating Independence Day, look through the window on the left-hand side. There is a Chinese restaurant across the street from John's house, but the real gem is the small sign advertising **Herb Ryman, Attorney at Law**. It's hard to read, but it's a tribute to Imagineer Herbert Ryman, concept artist who sketched the interior of the G.E. Carousel of Progress attraction for the 1964 New York World's Fair.

Fascinating Fact

The original version of the Carousel of Progress created for the 1964 New York World's Fair featured four eras: 1890, 1920, 1940, and the "modern day" of the 1960s. It was the first time Imagineers created Audio-Animatronic cats and dogs, and the first time Audio-Animatronic humans were used on a large scale. The characters' heads for the show were designed by sculptor Blaine Gibson, who used the face of Imagineer Dick Irvine's daughter as the model for the show's young daughter.

The final scene celebrating Christmas wouldn't be complete without a little something from Walt Disney World, and one lucky family member has a **large plush Mickey Mouse** waiting under the tree, to the left of Grandpa's rocking chair. Look carefully and you'll see the top of Mickey's head poking up from behind some wrapped gifts.

Mickey also appears as a **nutcracker on the mantle** at the far left side of the room, in an **abstract painting of sorcerer Mickey** behind the television set Grandma and Jimmy are using to play a video game, and as **salt and pepper grinders** on the kitchen counter. If you are sitting far enough to the right, you'll also see a Mickey cutout pasted to the gift next to Grandpa.

Imagine That!

Being a Disney Cast Member can be the most magical work experience in the world, but it comes with its challenges, too. Ron Rodriguez remembers one of Magic Kingdom's popular bands: "The Kids of the Kingdom band played the same show every day for years, and it could be maddening for them. Each year we had three weeks of rehearsal scheduled, but they already knew what to do so we wanted to play somewhere else when we weren't doing our regular playlist. There was a new parade at Magic Kingdom, and it was suggested they should ride on one of the floats to fill up their downtime. But these were musicians, not actors, and they didn't want to smile and wave. So I took three technicians instead, who dressed up and pretended to be musicians. Well, the Who's Who of Disney management was watching from the Hub, and when they saw the float the only person they recognized was me. When the parade ended I told those technicians to scatter, quick! The Kids of the Kingdom were allowed to branch out and play at the Tomorrowland Terrace after that."

Space Mountain

While you're in the queue, look for interplanetary route maps on the left-hand side. There are a few Disney references here, for **Disney's Hyperion Resort** and for the characters **Pluto** and **Ariel** who, not so coincidentally, are also a dwarf planet and a moon, respectively. Disney's Hyperion Resort is a reference to one of Walt Disney's studios and is also the name of one of Saturn's moons.

Just after you enter Space Mountain, take a look at the sign that lists various Earth Stations. **Tomorrowland Station MK-1** is the station here in Tomorrowland. MK refers to Orlando's Magic Kingdom and the numeral 1 indicates it was the first Space Mountain built in a Disney park. **TL Space Station 77** honors Disneyland's ride, which was built in 1977. **Discovery Landing Station—Paris** is Disneyland Paris's ride. There is no Tomorrowland in Paris, so the ride is located in Paris's Discoveryland. **Ashita Base—Tokyo** comes next, a reference to Tokyo Disneyland; *ashita* is Japanese for "tomorrow." And finally, **HK Spaceport E—TKT** is the space port in Hong Kong Disneyland. What does E—TKT stand for? Space Mountain was an E-ticket attraction when it opened at Magic Kingdom, meaning, your admission booklet (which had ticket designations A through E) allowed you the choice of one of eight "major" attractions per E-ticket. The term is now synonymous with "thrilling ride."

Once you're on the ride, pay attention (if you can!) as you make your way up the lift hill. The front of the spaceship suspended above you has the markings **H-NCH 1975**, a reference to Disney Legend John Hench, designer of the original Space Mountain, and to the year Spaceship Earth opened.

Although Magic Kingdom was not Walt Disney's primary intent for his great Florida project (that honor goes to the next park we'll explore), in terms of the historical timeline it had to come first. Profits from the park were necessary to raise the funding needed for Walt's true pet project, EPCOT Center. But from the perspective of the Show, Magic Kingdom comes in second to none. Open your eyes wide as you tour and imagine your own happy stories in this most magical of places!

Magic Kingdom Timeline

In 1958, the Walt Disney Company hired a private consultancy, Economics Research Associates, to begin a quest to find the ideal location where Walt could build his second theme park. The study indicated the obscure sites of Ocala and Orlando in Florida were most suited to the project. By 1963, Roy O. Disney and attorney Robert Foster proposed the purchase of 5,000 to 10,000 acres of land, prompting Walt to pay a visit to the area and make a final decision. After viewing the options, he settled on Orlando as the location for what would eventually become Walt Disney World.

Acting under the name Robert Price, Foster purchased 12,400 acres at a mere $107–$145 per acre, later adding another 9,750 acres at a relatively low cost. The total land purchase would span nearly 30,000 acres at a final cost of a little more than $5 million.

The *Orlando Sentinel* originally agreed not to reveal Disney's involvement in the land purchases, but, by the end of May 1965, the cat was nearly out of the bag. In June 1965, the *Orlando Evening Star* ran a feature referencing forty-seven transactions by Florida Ranch Lands, Inc., a boutique brokerage firm that was eventually revealed as working on behalf of Walt Disney in securing central Florida property. On October 25, Florida governor Haydon Burns confirmed Disney's purchase of the land and, on November 15, in the Cherry Plaza Hotel in Orlando, Walt, Roy, and Governor Burns formally announced plans to build the fledgling Disney resort.

Sadly, Walt never saw a single brick laid at the Florida location. He died of lung cancer on December 15, 1966. Roy O. Disney changed the name of the project from Disney World to Walt Disney World in honor of his brother, one of the great creative visionaries of the modern era. On May 30, 1967, ground broke for Magic Kingdom, "The Most Magical Place on Earth."

Opening Day 1971

The Magic Kingdom's grand opening took place on October 1, 1971, to a crowd of 10,000 visitors and at a cost of $400 million. Attractions open that day were **Cinderella's Golden Carrousel**, **Country Bear Jamboree**, **Diamond Horseshoe Revue**, **Dumbo the Flying Elephant**, **Frontierland Shootin' Arcade**, **Hall of Presidents**, **Haunted Mansion**, **it's a small world**, **Jungle Cruise**, **Mad Tea Party**, **Mickey Mouse Revue**, **Audio-Animatronics**, **Mike Fink Keel Boats**, **Mr. Toad's Wild Ride**, **Skyway to Tomorrowland** and **Skyway to Fantasyland**, **Snow White's Adventures**, **Swiss Family Treehouse**, **Tropical Serenade**, **Grand Prix Raceway**, and **Walt Disney World Railroad**. In addition, there were a full array of shops, dining options, a **Penny Arcade**, **House of Magic**, **Main Street Cinema**, various novelty vehicles, horse-drawn streetcars, and horseless carriages.

Admiral Joe Fowler **riverboat** opened on October 2, with **Peter Pan's Flight** debuting the next day. On October 14, **20,000 Leagues under the Sea** made its inaugural dive, and on Christmas Eve, the first guests blasted into outer space compliments of **Flight to the Moon**.

1971–1972: The Early Days

Admission into the park in 1971 was $3.50 for adults, $2.50 ages twelve to seventeen, and $1 ages three to eleven. Unlike today, guests then had a choice of two attraction tickets: an Adult 7-Attractions booklet ran $4.75. For an additional $1, adults could get an 11-Attractions booklet. Coupons allowed for one ride per coupon, from A-rides (such as Main Street Vehicles and Cinderella's Golden Carrousel) to E-rides (state-of-the-art attractions such as Haunted Mansion, Country Bear Jamboree, Jungle Cruise, and it's a small world).

Roy O. Disney presided over Magic Kingdom's dedication ceremony on October 23, 1971. In November, the **Electrical Water Pageant** parade made its first journey along Bay Lake while the Circle-Vision 360° film *America the Beautiful* debuted in Tomorrowland. December 1 saw the addition of a fourth locomotive, the *Roy O. Disney*.

Tragically, on December 20, Roy died of a cerebral hemorrhage. Control of Walt Disney World passed to Donn Tatum, acting as chairman, with Esmond Cardon "Card" Walker serving as president.

Eastern Airlines, the official airline of Walt Disney World, sponsored the **If You Had Wings** attraction in Tomorrowland, which opened on June 5, 1972, featuring a cutting-edge Omnimover ride system. By October 1, Walt Disney World's first anniversary, 10.7 million guests had passed through its gates.

1973–1974: Something New

The year 1973 saw a barrage of new attractions, including *The Walt Disney Story* in April, **Tom Sawyer Island**, **Tom Sawyer Island Rafts**, **Plaza Swan Boats**, and the *Richard F. Irvine riverboat* in May. But the most notable attraction debuted on December 15 when **Pirates of the Caribbean** opened in Adventureland. It would become a true Disney classic and go on to inspire a classic adventure movie series thirty years later.

America the Beautiful closed on March 15, 1974, reopening a day later with a new film, **Magic Carpet 'Round the World**, which lasted all of a year before being replaced by *America the Beautiful* again. **Star Jets**, the area's new centerpiece attraction, followed in November, providing a dizzying rocket-ride high above Tomorrowland.

By the end of 1974, Walt Disney World's popularity had grown to astonishing proportions. On December 29, a record 74,597 day-guests passed through the gates, causing the park to close due to capacity for the first time in its history.

1975: Liftoff for Tomorrowland

Long-awaited thrill-ride **Space Mountain** launched on January 15, 1975, adding a much-needed boost of adrenalin to an otherwise gentle park experience. Space travel remained very much in the public consciousness, though travel to the moon had lost some of its mystique. In response, Flight to the Moon became **Mission to Mars** on June 7, giving the attraction a new name and destination, although it remained essentially the same ride.

On June 6, **America on Parade** began running twice daily along Main Street's parade route in honor of the upcoming American Bicentennial.

A "great big beautiful tomorrow" arrived when the classic **Carousel of Progress** was moved from Disneyland in California to Magic Kingdom's Tomorrowland in 1975, with a new theme song, "The Best Time of Your Life." The original theme song would return in 1994, when the attraction was refurbished and renamed **Walt Disney's Carousel of Progress**.

1976–1981: Main Street Milestones

Although 1976 was quiet in terms of new attractions, the Magic Kingdom hit a milestone when day-guest Susan Brummer passed through the gates, achieving the distinction of being the park's 50 millionth visitor.

Destined to be a Disney classic, **Main Street Electrical Parade** premiered on June 11, 1977. It would grace Magic Kingdom twice, first for a fourteen-year run (1977–1991), and then again for two years (1999–2001).

The period from 1978 through mid-1980 was quiet at the Magic Kingdom as a second gate—EPCOT Center—broke ground in preparation for an October 1, 1982, opening. Mickey Mouse Revue closed at Magic Kingdom on September 14, 1980, followed by the retirement of the *Admiral Joe Fowler* riverboat. But big news came on November 8, with the opening of the park's second coaster, **Big Thunder Mountain Railroad**.

The Dream Called EPCOT film began showing at the EPCOT Preview Center in Magic Kingdom, generating excitement for the new park scheduled to open eleven years to the day after Magic Kingdom welcomed its first guests.

But 1981 also focused on Magic Kingdom's ten-year anniversary, with the stage show **Disney World Is Your World** and the **Tencennial Parade** running from October 1, 1981, through September 30, 1982, highlighting a celebration dubbed "a year long and a smile wide"—and smile wide, they did! Walt Disney World welcomed its 126 millionth guest during its Tencennial festivities.

1982–1983: The Quiet Year

Most of Walt Disney World's energy was focused on Epcot through 1982 and 1983; hence, the Magic Kingdom had to endure a quiet year. The graceful Plaza Swan Boats no longer swam the park's inland waters as of August 1983, victims of ongoing maintenance problems. However, their main docking area, a green-roofed platform next to the rose garden between the castle and Tomorrowland, could still be enjoyed as a shady rest area until 2014.

1984: A New Boss

A change in power occurred at Walt Disney World in 1984. Michael Eisner became the new chairman and chief executive officer following a major boardroom upheaval, with the company in the doldrums and losing money on both their theme park and film divisions. But the Magic Kingdom was not initially a primary focus for investment in new attractions.

A weak effort arrived in the form of the **Show Biz Is** show, which opened on July 12, 1984, only to close two months later. *America the Beautiful* was replaced by Circle-Vision 360° film **American Journeys**, while the new **Frontierland**

Shootin' Arcade offered little buckaroos the opportunity to spend a bit more of Mom and Dad's hard-earned cash on the chance to knock over a few prairie-themed targets. It was not a banner year.

1985–1987: More Development—But Not at Magic Kingdom

After the upheaval of 1984, it would take another four years before any new development occurred in Magic Kingdom. Time and money were focused on a rather quick decision to move forward with a third gate at Walt Disney World, the $300 million "Hollywood that never was and always will be" of Disney–MGM Studios.

In the meantime, **Merlin's Magic Shop** closed in Magic Kingdom in May 1986 and the Diamond Horseshoe Revue was renamed the **Diamond Horseshoe Jamboree**. Eastern Airlines was dropped as the If You Had Wings sponsor in January 1986. The name was changed to **If You Could Fly** on June 6. Capping off a rather uninspired year, *Magic Journeys*, the first in-park 3D effort by Walt Disney Imagineering, debuted at the Fantasyland Theater on December 15. The park would remain quiet throughout 1987, with no new attractions.

1988–1990: Junior Jamboree

The year 1988 would make up for the lack of investment in the park in the mid-1980s, especially for families with young children. **Mickey's Birthdayland** opened on June 18, originally intended to be a temporary land for the duration of Mickey's birthday celebration.

The area consisted of **Mickey's House**, **Grandma Duck's Petting Farm**, **Mickey's Playground**, and three circus-style tents with character meet-and-greets and two live shows, including highlight show **Minnie's Surprise Birthday Party**. One of the prime attractions was a cow living at Grandma Duck's farm named Minnie Moo, born with the classic tri-circle Mickey head on her side.

Ending an ongoing struggle to find its identity, If You Could Fly closed for the last time on January 3, 1989. Debuting in its place, **Delta Dreamflight** opened on June 26 and became a guest favorite for its pop-up-book style and the illusion of entering a jet engine.

Due to its enormous popularity with families, the decision was made to keep Mickey's Birthdayland. It closed on April 22, 1990, reopening on May 26 under the name **Mickey's Starland**, with *Minnie's Surprise Birthday Party* replaced by the **Mickey's Magical TV World** show. Cheap cutout storefronts were replaced by more substantial façades.

1991–1993: Parades—and a Big Splash

September 14, 1991, saw the last running of the popular nighttime Main Street Electrical Parade. It was replaced on October 1 by the visually magnificent **SpectroMagic**. The **Surprise Celebration Parade** ran each afternoon, beginning September 22.

It had been twelve years, though, since Magic Kingdom brought in a major attraction. Finally, in 1992, on July 17 (with a dedication ceremony on October 2), **Splash Mountain** generated screams of delight, with its gentle log flume ride through vignettes based on the 1946 film *Song of the South* culminating in a final 52-foot plunge with Br'er Rabbit, straight into the briar patch!

The Walt Disney Story closed on October 5, 1992, followed by Mission to Mars on October 4, 1993. The Hall of Presidents underwent a major refurbishment, adding President Bill Clinton to the lineup on November 18, 1993, with new narration by poet Maya Angelou, who recited her poem "On the Pulse of Morning" at President Clinton's January 20 inauguration.

Also in November, the Carousel of Progress reclaimed its original theme song, "There's a Great Big Beautiful Tomorrow." On December 1, *Magic Journeys* at the Fantasyland Theater was presented for the last time. A month later, *American Journeys* closed, followed by Surprise Celebration Parade and Star Jets.

1994: City of the Future

By 1994, Tomorrowland needed, and got, a major overhaul. It had begun to look dated, so in an effort to avoid that happening in the future, the Imagineers gave it a more general design, creating a "city of the future," with all the services of a major interplanetary metropolis.

In the process, the WEDWay PeopleMover adopted the name **Tomorrowland Transit Authority**, creating instant confusion for new visitors looking for the TTC (Transportation and Ticket Center). Despite the name change, many purists persisted in calling it the WEDWay. Even more distressing, the classic attraction 20,000 Leagues under the Sea closed, another victim of difficult maintenance.

1994–1995: Drama and Comedy

On July 8, 1994, ***The Legend of the Lion King*** show debuted in the former Mickey Mouse Revue theater, with a unique blend of animation from *The Lion King* movie, human-animal puppet performances, and some wonderful lighting effects. On November 21, 1994, **the Timekeeper** attraction with Circle-Vision 360° film ***From Time to Time*** opened in Tomorrowland's Transportarium, with voices by comic duo Robin Williams as the Timekeeper and Rhea Perlman as time-traveling camera droid 9-Eye.

The wonderfully hometown Penny Arcade and the House of Magic closed on March 19, 1995, and on April 7, the Diamond Horseshoe Jamboree returned to its original name, the Diamond Horseshoe Revue. On the heels of the major refurbishment of Tomorrowland, Star Jets was reborn as **Astro Orbiter**, with the central rocket tower being replaced by a futuristic orbiting-planets theme.

Flying in circles around Tomorrowland wasn't enough to hold teenagers' attention, so on June 20, 1995, the **ExtraTERRORestrial Alien Encounter** began scaring the daylights out of little Mouseketeers (and big ones). Incredibly innovative, Alien Encounter was the theme-park equivalent of a psychological thriller and ultimately proved too un-Disney-like, especially as a Magic Kingdom attraction.

1996–1997: Goofy for More

Mickey's Starland, now called **Mickey's Toontown Fair**, enjoyed an expansion in June 1996, adding kiddie coaster **The Barnstormer at Goofy's Wiseacre Farm** (which replaced Grandma Duck's Petting Farm) and **Toontown Hall of Fame**. The Grand Prix Raceway's track was shortened to make room for the added attractions in Toontown, reopening on September 28 as **Tomorrowland Speedway**. On the other side of the park, the *Richard F. Irvine* riverboat was rechristened the *Liberty Belle*.

One of Disney's Nine Old Men, animator and railroad enthusiast **Ward Kimball**, received the honor of a namesake fifth locomotive, which made its debut at Magic Kingdom on

March 1, 1997. That April, popular King Stefan's Banquet Hall restaurant was renamed **Cinderella's Royal Table**.

1998–1999: Silver Anniversary Stunner

After a May 17, 1997, accident dumped a boatload of guests into the Rivers of America at Disneyland California, the Mike Fink Keel Boats attraction there and in Orlando closed for good. Some Disney purists believed a more startling catastrophe occurred when Cinderella Castle was transformed into the **Cinderella Castle Cake** during Walt Disney World's 25th Anniversary Celebration in late 1996, and they were delighted to see the balloon-like covering removed in January 1998.

On the strength of three enormously popular movies, *Aladdin*, *The Lion King*, and *Toy Story*, the Tiki Room reopened as **the Enchanted Tiki Room—Under New Management**, with Jafar's (from *Aladdin*) screeching parrot Iago acting as joint host with *The Lion King*'s Zazu, while the brand-new **Buzz Lightyear's Space Ranger Spin** became an instant E-ticket hit. Sadly, September 7 saw the closing of a Disney classic, Mr. Toad's Wild Ride. Toady handed over the deed to his former home on June 5, 1999, when **The Many Adventures of Winnie the Pooh** arrived.

2000–2002: New Millennium, New Shows

The year 2001 added new entertainment to the park, hot on the heels of a major promotion for Walt Disney World's Millennium Celebration in 2000. These included *Cinderella's Surprise Celebration* stage show, the daily parade **Share a Dream Come True**, and the return of the nighttime parade **SpectroMagic**, which replaced Main Street Electrical Parade on April 2. Geared toward the Dumbo the Flying

Elephant crowd, **the Magic Carpets of Aladdin** provided a much-needed kiddie ride in Adventureland. On October 1, Disney's 100 Years of Magic celebration began, honoring the anniversary of Walt Disney's birth.

2003–2004: More Mickey and Friends

The 3D multisensory treat *Mickey's PhilharMagic* took over the former *Legend of the Lion King* theater in 2003, a year after *Lion King* closed. Nearby, the Diamond Horseshoe Revue closed, replaced by the ill-conceived **Goofy's Country Dancin' Jamboree**, a preschool free-for-all with Cowboy Goofy and Friends.

The poignantly beautiful **Wishes: A Magical Gathering of Disney Dreams** fireworks show lit up the sky for the first time on October 8, 2003, and four days later, the ExtraTERRORestrial Alien Encounter closed, a victim, perhaps, of its own success. The attraction set out to be terrifying—and did so in grand style.

Its replacement arrived on November 16, 2004, when the mischievous alien from the megahit movie *Lilo and Stitch* teleported to Magic Kingdom with his own show, **Stitch's Great Escape**. Preschoolers were frightened by it, elementary-age kids loved it, and many parents dubbed it "just plain gross."

2005–2007: Movie Makeovers

New attractions were not high on the list for 2005–2006, but Disney could not ignore a generational problem caused by the wild success of 2003's blockbuster movie *Pirates of the Caribbean: The Curse of the Black Pearl*. Youngsters clamored for the movie's star, played by the iconic Johnny Depp, prompting Audio-Animatronics of the inimitable Captain Jack Sparrow to be added to the Adventureland attraction.

In keeping with the trend of creating movie-inspired attractions, **the Laugh Floor Comedy Club** soft-opened briefly in December 2006, with one-eyed comedian Mike Wazowski of *Monsters, Inc.* movie fame acting as the show's Monster of Ceremonies. In December 2006 it was renamed **Monsters, Inc. Laugh Floor Comedy Club**, and finally **Monsters, Inc. Laugh Floor** in March 2007. The attraction did not generate the screams of laughter expected, though many guests found the show's acronym to be hilarious, as it was, unfortunately, also an obscene pop-culture cinematic reference.

Urban legend came full circle during a major Haunted Mansion overhaul in 2007, formally introducing the ghostly bride story line, which was not intended in the original design. Purists railed at the idea this classic attraction would be tampered with, but just as the Imagineers did a beautiful job in making Pirates of the Caribbean a more contemporary story without losing any of its original charm, so too did the Haunted Mansion's remake find favor. Some would argue it was better than ever!

2008–2014: Expanding the Fantasy

The years 2008 and 2009 were quiet, with rumors floating around about the next big thing coming to Magic Kingdom. By mid-2009 blueprints were leaked that showed a major Fantasyland expansion in the area occupied by a Winnie the Pooh playground, the former 20,000 Leagues under the Sea attraction, and Toontown. While most of the plan's attractions came into being, some, including Pixie Hollow, fell by the wayside.

With an estimated five-year span before the expansion would be realized, very little happened to breathe new life into the park. The long-running parade **SpectroMagic** ended June 5, 2010, and was replaced by **Main Street Electrical Parade** the next day. Seven months later a small fire occurred at **the Enchanted Tiki Room—Under New Management!** on January 12, 2011, closing the attraction. On August 15, 2011, the original version returned, effectively doing what millions of visitors wished they could do: bump off that annoying bird, Iago.

The Haunted Mansion's queue was extended, giving guests the option of a detour through an interactive graveyard, which opened in March 2011. The augmented "hitchhiking ghosts" scene at the end of the attraction began on April 4, 2011, and after the successful addition of Captain Jack Sparrow and other characters from the hit movie series, mermaids from *Pirates of the Caribbean: On Stranger Tides* were added to the Adventureland attraction in October 2012.

Mickey's Toontown Fair closed permanently on February 11, 2011, as part of the Fantasyland expansion plans, and on March 12, 2012, Goofy's Barnstormer at Wiseacre Farm reopened as the Barnstormer featuring Goofy as the Great Goofini. Dumbo the Flying Elephant was relocated from Fantasyland to Storybook Circus (formerly Toontown), reopening on March 12, 2012. A second Dumbo opened next to it, in July 2012. The remainder of Storybook Circus, including Casey Jr. Splash 'n' Soak Station, opened in July 2012.

Enchanted Tales with Belle and **Under the Sea: Journey of the Little Mermaid** opened December 6, 2012, as a debut of the addition to Fantasyland, nicknamed Fantasyland Forest.

Princess Fairytale Hall meet-and-greet began receiving visitors on September 18, 2013, and the final element of the Fantasyland expansion, **Seven Dwarfs Mine Train**, opened May 28, 2014, adding a sense of kinetic excitement to the most magical land in the park.

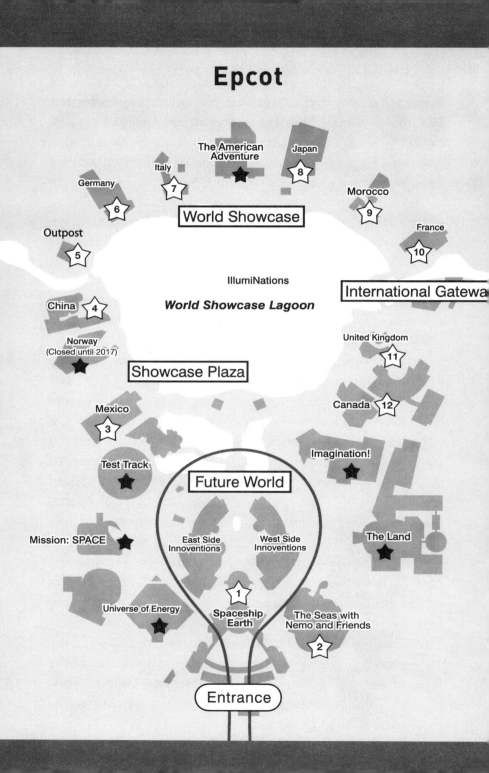

1. **Spaceship Earth:** The Cro-Magnon scene at the beginning of your journey includes the skulls of a saber-toothed cat, a bear, a lion, and two wolves. They are replicas of real skulls from a collection at the Page Museum in Los Angeles.

2. **The Seas with Nemo & Friends:** The advertisement for Daily Diving Departures at The Seas with Nemo & Friends are provided by Nautical Exploration and Marine Observation, or NEMO.

3. **Mexico:** What's so important about the round stone tablet in the middle of the lobby area that leads to the Plaza de los Amigos? It's a replica of an Aztec calendar.

4. **China:** Enter the House of Good Fortune and look down at the floor. The design mimics a bridge over a lotus pond, and if you listen closely you'll hear birdsong.

5. **Outpost:** Along with Korean and Russian, look for the Chinese markings on a red cooler which, loosely translated, mean "let me treat you to a drink."

6. **Germany:** The painting on the wall opposite the Sommerfest features the famous Rothenburg ob der Tauber, considered one of Germany's most romantically styled villages. In reality, the painting covers what would have been the entry to a never-built Rhine River cruise attraction.

7. **Italy:** The bridge behind the Doge's Palace represents the infamous Bridge of Sighs that convicts would have crossed on their way to the palace's prison.

8. **Japan:** The stone lantern in the landscaping in front Mitsukoshi was given to Roy O. Disney by the Japanese government to honor the opening of the Japan pavilion in 1982.

9. **Morocco:** Inside Tangier Traders shop is a pretty wooden board that looks like a work of art. Moroccan Cast Members doing their international internship program at Epcot sign their names on it in Arabic.

10. **France:** Les Halles counter service area is based on the Parisian fresh-food market of the same name, while the exterior, the seating area, and the gift shop are designed to look like a typical French train station.

11. **United Kingdom:** The façade of the Sportsman's Shoppe is based on a small section of Scottish author Sir Walter Scott's Abbotsford House.

12. **Canada:** Only one of the totem poles in the Canada pavilion is real. It depicts a traditional Raven story, one of many told by the Tsimshian people.

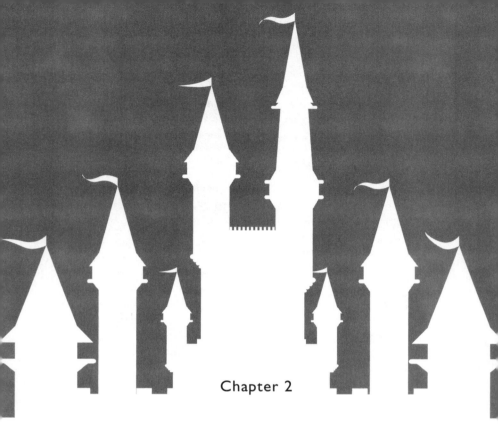

Chapter 2

Epcot

After the world journey of Magic Kingdom, Walt Disney World's second park comes as a complete change, focusing on the human journey toward invention, inspiration, and cooperation.

Epcot, the **Experimental Prototype Community of Tomorrow**, is a celebration of life, diversity, and the possibilities held by countless tomorrows. It is first and foremost a park dedicated to discovery, anticipation of a world bettered by technology, revelations of humankind's differences, and more important, our similarities.

Walt Disney did not live to see even the beginning of the creation of the park, originally called EPCOT Center when it opened on October 1, 1982. But his plans for Epcot detailed his vision of a self-contained community with all peoples working in harmony toward the common goal of a better world. Walt expressed this vision in the **City of the Future** model, which can be seen while riding Magic Kingdom's Tomorrowland Transit Authority. Epcot would be a dynamic community, ever growing and changing to reflect the ongoing process of human and technological progress.

After Walt's death in 1966, the plans for Epcot divided it into two separate, distinct parks, one showcasing the latest technology and the second a tribute to world cultures. After much grumbling and debate between the designers, Imagineer John Hench took the two park models, which were sitting near each other on a design table, and literally pulled everything together. From this one small act, a brand-new Walt Disney World theme park was born. And now, we have Epcot!

The lure of Spaceship Earth is strong, but pause for a moment before you rush headlong into the park. Just outside the turnstiles, at the base of the flagpole, you'll find **Epcot's dedication plaque** with CEO E. Card Walker's comments on the official park opening day of October 24, 1982, though the park actually opened on October 1.

Future World

Future World represents both the living world on the right side of the park and the world of innovation on the left, separated by Innoventions Plaza and the Fountain of Nations. Notice the smooth, curved lines of the curbs, pathways, rocks, and landscaping on the right side of Future World and the more angular, well-defined lines on the left? Making the distinction between nature's flow and science's requirement to operate within specific lines is a small design element that enhances the complete theme. This distinction can even be extended to the human brain, with the right side of the park representing creative right-brain thinking and the left side of the park reflecting the more linear nature of the left brain's functions.

Imagine That!

Gene Columbus, former Manager of Magic Kingdom Entertainment, was instrumental in organizing the grand opening ceremony at Epcot, and recalls some of the challenges prior to the park's debut. He says, "I was assigned to work on the grand opening of EPCOT Center with my primary duty to be the dedication. Leading up to this event there were a number of walk-throughs of the construction site. Trucks and earthmovers were everywhere, so the site had planks of wood laid down for us to get from place to place. This is Florida and a swamp, with the ground mainly of wet muck! As we planned the events we needed to take folks out to see the space and it was my job to take them on tours. Keep in mind that this was a time in which we wore ties and often jackets, but hardhats were also required. I would tell the group where things were and what was going on in each location, and at times I would walk backward to ensure they could hear me as well as making sure we were all looking at what we needed to see. The challenge was that if you stepped off the plank in the muck, it was not pretty. I did, and the muck sucked my shoe off my foot! I finished the tour promising myself never to let that happen again. A couple of weeks later I was doing a tour, and near the location of my first encounter it happened again. In both cases it was my left shoe. Over the years I've thought it would be interesting that thousands of years from now when someone digs in this area they will find these two shoes and conclude that people of this period in human development had two left feet, and to tell the difference they wore shoes of different colors."

In keeping with the spirit of a global community, the Innoventions Plaza's Fountain of Nations (known as Fountain of World Friendship when Epcot opened) contains water from **rivers and bodies of water** around the world, with a gallon from each having been added to the fountain on opening day as a gesture of peace and togetherness.

Fascinating Fact

Curious about which bodies of water were included in the International Ceremony of the Waters? The water came from the Adriatic Sea, the Arctic Ocean, the Bodensee (which represents Switzerland, Germany, and Austria), the Caribbean Sea, the Cauca River in Colombia, an underground river in Korea, a sample of God's Water from the Ise Grand Shrine near Osaka, Harrison's Cave water from Barbados, Lake Geneva, Lake Inari in Finland, the Manzanares River in Spain, the Meuse River (which runs through France, Belgium, and the Netherlands), mineral springs water of Sidi Ali in Morocco, the Mississippi and Nile Rivers, the Philippine Sea, the River Thames, the Sea of Japan, the Seine, Senegambia River, Tivoli Gardens Lake in Denmark, Trevi Fountain in Rome, Lake Xochimilco in Mexico City, the Yangtze River, and a dam in the former Czechoslovakia.

Spaceship Earth

The Imagineers strive to communicate their story effectively, making the attractions themselves a virtual playground of hidden magic. In the case of Spaceship Earth, the story is about communication and human innovation.

You won't notice it as you move through Spaceship Earth, but the **geodesic sphere** is actually two pieces: the outer shell, and an inner shell through which the ride vehicles travel.

The Imagineers spared no effort in creating accurate scenes inside Spaceship Earth, right down to re-creating some of the actual musical instruments, documents, and machines that add an extra air of authenticity. In the Sistine Chapel scene, Michelangelo's **paint conveyer system** is a replica of the original, and the **steam press** in the printing scene is a duplicate of a press designed by William Bullock in 1863. In fact, nearly every key item in Spaceship Earth is a replica of a real historical artifact.

It's obvious you're meant to be traveling through time, but take note of the transitions as you wind through Spaceship Earth. The story starts with prehistory, moves on to ancient history, medieval times, the Renaissance, and finally, the modern era, starting with the mid-1860s and the end of the American Civil War. Milestones in American history then take riders through to the late 1970s and the invention of the home computer before turning toward a glimpse at the future. There is a sudden shift in focus from world events to U.S. milestones, a subtle tribute to the impact the United States has had upon the world.

The Cro-Magnon scene at the beginning of your journey includes the **skulls** of a saber-toothed cat, a bear, a lion, and two wolves. They are replicas of real skulls from a collection at the Page Museum in Los Angeles.

The Cro-Magnon sequence may seem rather simple, but it's a beautiful example of the attraction's theme. It expresses the drive to communicate through the **shaman's storytelling**, the **cave-dwellers' wall art**, and even in the **body language of the hunters** fighting off the mastodon. Each of these elements was inspired by Disney's Magic Skyway exhibit in the 1964 New York World's Fair.

The scrolls in the Egyptian scene duplicate real **documents written by a pharaoh** to one of his agents. If you've brushed up on hieroglyphic writing, you'll know the **hieroglyphics** throughout the Egyptian scene are accurate representations of real words.

Although the smell of burning wood may distract you, notice the graffiti on the walls as you pass by the sacking of Rome scene. It reproduces actual **graffiti** found in the Roman city of Pompeii.

Next up is the Renaissance. While guests will never have the opportunity to try it out, the movable type on the **printing press** in the scene really can move. Johann Gutenberg would also be delighted to know his likeness in the same scene is reading an exact reproduction of the original forty-two-line Gutenberg Bible. The page depicted in Spaceship Earth copies an original housed at the Huntington Library in San Marino, California. Why the forty-two-line distinction? It refers to how many lines were printed on each page, not that the entire Bible consisted of only forty-two lines.

As you continue to spiral upward through Spaceship Earth, listen closely as you pass by the telegraph scene. Can you hear **Morse code**? The message being tapped out is the 1869 announcement that the golden spike linking the transcontinental railway at Promontory Peak has just been driven in.

The newspaper you see in the scene with the steam printing press isn't the **New York Daily** (notice the letters are not correct, even as an anagram), but it is meant to make you think of that paper in the same way the symbol on the airplane in *Indiana Jones Epic Stunt Spectacular* is not a Nazi swastika, but fools your eye into thinking it is.

When you reach the switchboard scene, take notice of the **magneto switchboard** with operators plugging cord circuits into connectors. It is based on an 1898 model by AT&T, Spaceship Earth's sponsor from 1986 until 2003. The telephone in the Chapeau at Magic Kingdom is also a form of magneto telephone service.

Who is that **computer guy** sitting in the garage, inventing the personal computer? Think he might be Microsoft's Bill Gates or Apple's Steve Jobs or Steve Wozniak? Nope. The official Imagineer stance is that he is a compilation of everyone whose efforts went into creating PCs.

Imagine That!

Pam Fisher, Walt Disney Imagineer and senior show writer, says the garage scene is "an homage to all the young dreamers working out of their garages and on their kitchen tables, perfecting all the technologies needed to create the personal computer. Hewlett-Packard started in a garage. Apple started in a garage. But there were also many other nameless people in Northern California working in their own garages at the time, figuring out the other parts of the puzzle. This scene is a salute to them all."

Universe of Energy

Turning to the left, or scientific, side of Future World, the Universe of Energy may be the most obviously educational attraction in Walt Disney World. It was originally a rather dry litany of potential energy sources, making the ride popular for a nap in air-conditioned comfort. Now it's an engaging look at the world's energy options as seen by comedian Ellen DeGeneres and her good friend Bill Nye the Science Guy.

As you approach Universe of Energy, notice how the vertical columns are reminiscent of a **rainbow**. Before the pavilion's 1996 makeover, the color scheme was more in keeping with the energy theme, with panels running along each side starting as a warm sunshine yellow, gradually becoming fiery umber, like a beacon pointing toward a red-hot power center.

In fact, that red-hot center originally represented **volcanic lava flow**. A curiosity here is that if you start at the wide, "cool" ends on either side of the pavilion and move to the pointy, "hot" ends, the shape it creates fits within the shape of the "lava flow" pathway you'll see at the Land pavilion.

The pavilion's icon is composed of two structures, the **Trylon** (spire) and the **Perisphere** (the round part skewered on the Trylon). These two elements were originally separate and were the icon of the 1939 World's Fair in New York.

Fans of the 1940 Disney movie *Fantasia* might recognize a small tribute to Walt's most ambitious cinematic undertaking as they travel past a confrontation between the *T. rex* and stegosaurus. The same scene can be found in the movie's *Rite of Spring* composition, depicting the creation of the cosmos through to the dinosaurs' extinction.

The *T. rex* and stegosaurus fight scene was based on the segment in *Fantasia*, but the Audio-Animatronic version in Universe of Energy originally featured in Disney's Magic Skyway exhibit at the 1964 New York World's Fair. A version of the brontosaurus scene and the pterodactyl scene also debuted at the fair.

As you exit the dinosaur portion of the ride, you hear a radio broadcast compliments of **KNRG News Radio**. Do the station's call letters bring anything to mind? They are a shortened version of "kinetic energy."

Mission: SPACE

The next pavilion, Mission: SPACE, holds the secret to space travel, providing an experience the average person could not have any other way. When the attraction originally opened, it was too much like the real thing. Although it was toned down, it remains the only attraction in Orlando equipped with motion discomfort bags.

Mission: SPACE is loosely based on the 1955 movie *Man in Space*, written, directed, and produced by Disney Legend Ward Kimball.

As you approach the pavilion, take a look at the pavement and see if you can spot the **asteroids** (hint: they have long tails).

Take time to look around the Planetary Plaza (courtyard) before you enter. The walls are adorned with **plaques containing quotes** from well-known astronomers and astronauts, including Kalpana Chawla, one of the astronauts who died in the tragic explosion of the *Columbia* space shuttle in 2003.

The **gold spheres** scattered across the mockup of the moon in the Planetary Plaza represent each of the twenty-nine moon-landing missions sent up by the United States and the Soviet Union between 1959 and 1976.

Before you head off on your training mission to Mars, listen to the announcements in the courtyard. You'll hear part of President John F. Kennedy's **"We choose to go to the moon, not because it is easy but because it is hard"** speech; the countdown you hear is from the **STS-7 space shuttle *Challenger* launch** with astronaut Sally Ride, the first American woman in space; and you'll hear "**Welcome**

to the International Space Training Center" in Italian, Chinese, and Russian.

While you're in the courtyard, look for a plaque embedded in an oval of red dirt. Within the context of the story, they were made by the Mars exploration rovers, *Spirit* and *Opportunity*. *Spirit* landed on Mars on January 4, 2004, and *Opportunity* landed on January 25, 2004. **Sean O'Keefe** was the NASA administrator who implemented the MER mission.

Fascinating Fact

On April 6, 2004, Sean O'Keefe and a group of NASA scientists and mission managers attended a ceremony at Epcot, accompanied by a Mars exploration rover, which made a ceremonial pass over the red dirt (which is really cement) now embedded in the courtyard at Mission: SPACE. This little plot of Red Planet celebrates the accomplishments of the rovers *Spirit* and *Opportunity*, including the discovery of evidence that indicates the surface of Mars once held water.

See that **Horizons logo** in the center of the rotating gravity wheel in the queue? Horizons was the name of the attraction located on the site that now houses Mission: SPACE. It centered on possible future habitat options in the harsh environments of the desert, the ocean, and space.

Once in the Training Ops bay, you will see **Mission Control** on the right. Imagineers are both creative and economical, using retired attraction set pieces if they fit into a new attraction. Mission: SPACE has a number of pieces from the old Mission to Mars ride, formerly in Tomorrowland at Magic Kingdom. The controls, switches, lights, and monitors are all recycled from the former attraction. The gravity wheel is from the 2000 movie *Mission to Mars*.

How did Disney decide what the Red Planet would look like during the landing portion of the ride? They contacted NASA's Jet Propulsion Lab for **satellite imagery of Mars' surface**. But that's not all they consulted with NASA about. The design of the **X-2 trainer** stems from scientific projections for future space travel; the **Ready Room** at Mission: SPACE is based on Kennedy Space Center's "White Room," where NASA astronauts waited before boarding their spacecraft; and the Mars landscape in the computer game **Expedition: Mars** in the post-show area's Advanced Training Lab contains imagery based on information provided by NASA.

After your successful training expedition, turn your hand to the interactive post-show elements, remembering to send yourself a postcard from space. While you're waiting for your turn to play some of the simulator games, take a peek in the cabinet on the left side of the alcove you will see as you walk through. The little yellow book titled *Expedition: Mars Noctis Labyrinthus* refers to the Noctis Labyrinthus, or "labyrinth of the night," which is a complex of winding valleys on Mars.

Imagine That!

Developing attraction concepts isn't as simple as coming up with a terrific idea, especially when it requires new technology and financial backing. Mission: SPACE was one such attraction. Imagineer Eddie Sotto, Senior Vice President of Concept Design with Walt Disney Imagineering from 1986 to 1999, describes the process when he says the Imagineers wanted to "give the most accurate ride experience that would simulate a rocket launch, as that was what most guests were fascinated with when it came to space. The funny thing about Mission: SPACE is that we really wanted management to know the ride experience was going to be unique. In order to get the funding to convince them, I had to lie on my back suspended between two chairs, facing the ceiling, making all manner of 'communications chatter' and engine noises, contorting my face to simulate the sustained g-forces on my body, all in a business suit. Think Cirque du Soleil meets *Apollo 13*. Marty Sklar, WDI's president, enthusiastically decided to fund the development of the show, but thankfully never asked me to demonstrate the effect again!"

Test Track

Test Track underwent a massive makeover in 2012 as sponsorship of the pavilion transitioned from General Motors to the Chevrolet Division of General Motors. The track remains the same, but the proving-grounds theme was removed and now guests enter a **Chevrolet design center** where they can create and test their own cars inside a computer-driven environment that looks remarkably similar to the Walt Disney Pictures movie *Tron*. While all the whimsical hidden magic of the previous ride was removed, there are still a few little gems to look for as you make your way through the digital world of this virtual testing ground.

Enter the queue and you're in a Chevrolet Design Center complete with concept cars, then it's on to the studio where riders can design their own cars based on Capability, Responsiveness, Efficiency, and Power. But the real fun begins when you board a test car and take "your" design for a spin on the Sim Track. And this is where a bit of hidden magic can be found.

As you reach the first bend after the glowing pine trees, look to your right. You'll see what looks like a School Crossing sign with **two people crossing a road holding**

an artists' palette. They are based on the profiles of two engineers who worked on the attraction.

Imagine That!

Imagineer Melissa Jeselnick points out a little-known secret in Test Track: "We have actual items, sketches, cars, and models from General Motors that have never been seen before by anyone outside the Chevrolet family."

Just after your OnStar guide says, "Okay, the Responsiveness data is now being synchronized," watch for a **three-tiered road sign** on the left-hand side of the track that points to Motion Lane, General Motorway, and Bowtie Boulevard, all nods to the experience and the attraction's sponsors.

Shortly after your OnStar guide says, "Automated driving technology verified and active," watch for a sign on the right-hand side of the track with a character that looks like a squirrel but is actually a **beaver**. It is a reference to Big Beaver Road in Troy Michigan, a General Motors branch location and the workplace of many of the employees who helped design the attraction.

Innoventions Plaza

Back in the center of Future World, Electric Umbrella is a great place for a quick lunch or a drink to beat the heat. Be sure to throw your rubbish in the trash bin marked **Waste Please** (usually next to the toppings bar where the condiments and burger fixings are located). Listen closely for a surprising commentary; you may hear children arguing over who gets the last of the fries!

Birds of the aggressive variety used to frequent the Walt Disney World outdoor dining locations. Why are they less pervasive at Epcot now? It is said the speaker systems play sounds of **birds in distress**, which keep hungry winged pests at bay. Many outdoor locations also use coverings or wires to discourage bird invasion, so although places like Electric Umbrella have nicely shaded outdoor dining, it's really there to keep the birds away.

Remember the right-brain/left-brain analogy as it relates to each side of Future World? Further references can be seen around the pin-trading kiosk where visitors can buy, sell, and trade Disney lapel pins. Look around the kiosk; the circles on the ground represent the **right brain's flowing nature** while the design of the awnings represents **linear left-brain thinking**.

Pass through the walkway between Innoventions West and Epcot Character Spot, heading toward the Land pavilion. Just beyond, you'll take a "walk through time" over the **Timeline of Discovery**. Look at the large circle below your feet with quotations from various scientists and inventors about their reflections on historical discoveries, such as the Phoenician invention of the alphabet, Heinrich Hertz's discovery of radio waves, the creation of the internal combustion engine by Jean-Joseph Étienne Lenoir, and the discovery of penicillin by Alexander Fleming.

Imagine That!

Disney Legend Ron Logan was a member of the team that created Epcot. He recalls hosting a media preview while the park was under construction, taking journalists through what was then mostly scrubland: "We got a big flatbed truck and put a band on it, which we called the Hardhat Orchestra, who played as we took the media to the place where Spaceship Earth was going to go. All the pavilions were marked with balloons. When my driver arrived to pick me up I noticed he had all these flea collars around his ankles. When I asked him what they were for he just said, 'You'll find out.' The whole area was covered in mud, with mosquitoes and snakes everywhere. We had to carry machetes when we worked in there. It was like a jungle!"

The Land

Crossing over to the nature-based side of Future World, the Land pavilion draws guests in with sweeping mosaics along both sides of the walkway. The artist designed the mosaics as representations of the **layers of the earth**, exposed after a volcanic eruption.

The mural running along each side of the walkway to the entry represents **sixty different natural materials**, including gold, granite, and pumice.

Also notice the walkway as you make your way up to the pavilion's door. The pigmented pavement is an extension of the theme—in this case, of the creation of land—and is meant to represent **lava** flowing from a volcano. The red pavement is hot lava; the black is cooled lava.

Fascinating Fact

All the natural elements that went into creating the murals at the Land pavilion's entrance were made from materials found on Walt Disney World property.

Living with the Land

In keeping with Walt's vision for his city of tomorrow, **quotations** adorning the wall along the queue for the Living with the Land ride offer eloquent insights into humankind's relationship with the environment. As profound as they are, each quotation comes from the unique perspective of the children who wrote them. These quotations come from children around the world, some as young as five years old!

During your boat ride, note the **house number** on the mailbox as you pass through the farmhouse scene on the ride. It's number 82, a subtle nod to 1982, the year Epcot opened.

Fascinating Fact

Plants in the Living with the Land greenhouses are grown using a soil-free technique called hydroponics (*hydro* meaning "water" and *ponic* meaning "labor"). It seems like a high-tech method, but it has been around for centuries. Ancient hieroglyphs show the Egyptians grew plants in water; the Aztecs and Chinese created floating gardens; the Hanging Gardens of Babylon used hydroponics; World War II troops stationed in the Pacific without usable soil were fed partially through hydroponic systems; and later, even NASA got in on the act.

If you dine at Sunshine Seasons food court, choose one of the single-serving side dishes that rest on a lettuce leaf and you're guaranteed to be dining on lettuce grown in the Living with the Land attraction.

Soarin'

The pavilion's other big attraction, Soarin', was originally built at Disney's California Adventure park in Anaheim in 2001. As you watch the preflight video, notice the **flight number**. It is 5505, honoring the official opening of Soarin' at Epcot on May 5, 2005.

Although you'll be soaring over California and you're actually in Florida, the airport at Soarin' is based on **Charles de Gaulle Airport** in Paris, France.

As you walk through the queue, notice how **the ceiling represents the sky**, with clouds floating by. If you watch closely, the light will dim just a bit each time a cloud goes by.

Pay attention to the queue's **metal walls**. The screen for Soarin' is made of the same material.

If you think the actors in the show are Disney Imagineers, you're right. While each scene looks completely natural, if you watch closely you'll see certain actors are clearly waiting for their cue. In particular, pay attention to the way the **Redwood Creek fly fisherman** pauses as he casts, and to the unfortunate **Lake Tahoe skier's** jump, timed perfectly so that his fall is captured as your hang glider passes by.

Why is the San Diego scene so blurry in comparison to the rest of the film? As you would imagine, Disney needed special permission to make a pass over the **aircraft carrier**, and to their dismay the videographers discovered the first take wasn't ideal. However, they could not get permission for a second pass, so the original video sequence remains.

The Seas with Nemo & Friends

As you walk through the queue toward your "clamobile," notice the **beach signs** on the tall white signpost. If you look carefully at the advertisement for Daily Diving Departures, you will notice they are provided by Nautical Exploration and Marine Observation, or NEMO.

The **Tanks a Lot Dive Shop** is the place to rent diving equipment while you're visiting Coral Caves Beach, and its street address holds a special meaning. It is a reference to

Walt Disney Imagineering's address, 1401 Flower Street in Glendale, California.

Imagination!

As you make your way toward World Showcase, you'll find the last of the Future World pavilions, Imagination! This pavilion is all about whimsy and the strange and wonderful places our imagination can take us with "just one spark."

Never satisfied with the obvious when a bit of ingenuity could be employed, the Imagineers have taken a twist on the waterfall concept. Look at the **water feature** as you walk toward the pavilion. The water isn't flowing downward; it's shooting upward, a mental nudge to viewers to allow their creativity to run wild.

Journey into Imagination with Figment

Check out the names on the doors as you walk through the Imagination Institute. **Dean Finder** is a reference to Dreamfinder, the original host of the Imagination pavilion. **Professor Wayne Szalinski** is from the movie *Honey, I Shrunk the Kids*, which had a spinoff attraction, Honey, I Shrunk the Audience, at the Imagination pavilion from 1994 to 2010. **Professor Philip Brainard** is from the movies *The Absent-Minded Professor* and its retelling, *Flubber*. Here it refers specifically to *Flubber*, as evidenced by the picture of Robin Williams as Professor Brainard, located in the institute's lobby. **Dean Higgins** is from the series of movies that were set in Medfield College, as is **Dr. Nigel Channing**, played by the actor Eric Idle of *Monty Python's Flying Circus* fame.

Stop for a moment or two when you reach Dr. Channing's office. His **harried secretary** is struggling to keep up with Dr. Channing's phone calls, with hilarious results!

You'll hear several **humorous announcements** over the intercom as you make your way to the attraction's boarding area. Listen for the comment, "Attention Dexter Riley. Please bring your tennis shoes to the Smell Lab." Dexter Riley is from the 1969 Walt Disney Company movie *The Computer Wore Tennis Shoes*. It seems Dexter heard the announcement. When you reach the Smell Lab you'll see his **tennis shoes** sitting outside the door.

You'll also see Dexter's **Medfield College letterman jacket** in the Smell Lab. It is a reference to several Walt Disney Company movies in which Medfield College features, including *The Computer Wore Tennis Shoes*, *The Absent-Minded Professor*, and *Flubber*.

Notice the artwork in Figment's house. Two portraits are the dragon version of the famous **Blue Boy** and **Pink Girl** paintings.

When Cast Members are hired they go through a training session called **Disney Traditions**, and some attractions have a place where new CMs can add their name after their training is over. Just before you reach the Touch and Taste Lab, you'll see an open book on the table to the right of the bay door, on your right-hand side. It is Imagination's **CM signature book**.

The **cartoon-style images** in the final reveal at the end of the ride are a nod to the pavilion's former attraction, Journey into Imagination, with beloved characters Figment and Dreamfinder.

Imagine That!

Gene Columbus, former Manager of Entertainment Staffing, talks about a memorable event he and his team planned, and how the job of all Disney Leaders is to make it look easy if things go wrong: "Many years ago we were hosting the International Chamber of Commerce and the keynote speaker was President Jimmy Carter. This black-tie event in the Magic Kingdom was spectacular, with a full orchestra performing *Fanfare for the Common Man* by Aaron Copland as the preshow. I was on a headset calling cues, but was also connected to Disney Security because of all the Secret Service protocol. They also gave me updates on the weather because a large rainstorm was heading toward the Magic Kingdom. While the president of the United States is speaking no one moves, and we had a symphony orchestra sitting right in front of where he was to speak. Priceless stringed instruments and woodwinds as well as a grand piano and two harps were very much at risk. Secret Service would not agree to our request to have the musicians leave or get the instrument cases, but as a compromise they let us send a stage crew member on his hands and knees to give the musicians garbage bags for their instruments when it started raining. President Carter was to speak for ten to twelve minutes and then we had a huge finale with more than a hundred beautifully costumed performers with silk banners. I put everyone on standby saying if it was not raining at the moment the president concluded his remarks we would move forward with the big finale of dancing waters, fireworks, balloons, and doves flying overhead. Moments after I gave the 'GO!' the rain started, and with it high winds. The performers were now on stage and the fireworks smoke blew into the audience so they could not see the stage. However, while I was dealing with the garbage bags, the members of the Guest Relations team got umbrellas—hundreds of them—and had a line of Disney Cast Members on their knees passing them out to the guests. As if on cue, the hundreds of umbrellas opened and guests headed for the shops on Main Street, U.S.A., where they enjoyed the rest of the party. The orchestra members made a run for it while the performers kept going, even without music, and got soaked to the skin. No doubt a number of costumes were ruined, as were all the silk banners. Disney had to replace the two harps and the grand piano was never the same. When talking to guests about their experience they were amazed at many things, but what stuck out most was the moment the umbrellas opened. After the guests left the area and were inside, I stood there for a few minutes completely soaked and what I remember most was watching a lighting tree fall over, smashing a couple of chairs. No one was hurt, but that caused us to have many safety meetings on how that happened!"

World Showcase

The layout of the international pavilions that make up this half of the park is well established. The original concept placed the U.S.A. pavilion at the front of World Showcase (in what is now Showcase Plaza) with near-neighbors Mexico and Canada bordering on either side. Guests would walk through an archway into World Showcase, with the main attraction, the American Adventure, housed in a building situated above the archway. Ultimately it was decided America should "play host to the World," and the pavilion was centered at the back. Mexico and Canada remain in their original positions.

Imagine That!

Even relatively straightforward attractions like a parade have their challenges. Disney Legend Ron Logan recalls, "Michael Eisner wanted us to come up with a parade for Epcot, which is when we created Tapestry of Nations. The big challenge was that you can see across the lagoon, so if you're in Mexico you can see the parade in the United Kingdom, but it would take twenty minutes for it to get to you, and by then you would be bored with it already. We made the parade so that it started in three places. No matter where you were, you would see it right away."

A curiosity as you walk toward Mexico from Showcase Plaza again highlights the attention to detail Disney Imagineers bring to their work. Once you pass the shop in Showcase Plaza, begin looking toward the Morocco pavilion. Does something look slightly out of place? What appears to be a Moroccan building far off in the distance is actually the top of the **Tower of Terror** at Disney's Hollywood Studios. When the Imagineers realized you could see the tower from Epcot, they included stylized minarets on the roof to help the tower blend more harmoniously with the Moroccan theme.

Mexico

As authentic as it looks at first glance, the Mexico pavilion's pyramid actually represents three distinct cultures. The pyramid architecture is **Mayan**, with one temple built at the top rather than two, as would be seen on an Aztec pyramid. The decor is **Aztec**, with brightly colored murals and menacing heads guarding the entry. Many of the design elements throughout are representative of **Toltec** art. The pyramid itself is a representation of an **Aztec temple of Quetzalcoatl.** Each serpent head symbolizes Quetzalcoatl, son of the Creator God.

Two ecosystems are represented in the Mexico pavilion. On the pyramid side of the pavilion you're in Mexico's **verdant jungle**. Cross the pavement to La Hacienda and La Cantina de San Angel and you've reached Mexico's **barren desert of the Pacific Northwest**.

Why is it always **twilight inside Mexico's Plaza de los Amigos**, which is based on the town of Taxco? Because twilight is the time friends and family—relationships central to Mexican culture—gather in the plaza for socializing.

Animales fantásticos, the **colorful wooden figures** being carved inside the pavilion, are an ancestral Zapotec art form in Oaxaca (pronounced "Wa-HAH-ca"), Mexico. Known as *alebrijes*, the magical creatures hold a special secret. Because the artist puts such intense effort into the work, it is believed the piece carries part of the carver's being forever.

As you stand in front of La Hacienda, notice the **birds perched on the bars** across the upper-story windows. It's a pretty little detail that adds a lifelike touch to the building.

Once you enter the pavilion, you can't miss the enormous **round stone tablet** in the middle of the lobby area that leads to the Plaza de los Amigos, but what's so important about it that it deserves such a prominent placement? It's a replica of an **Aztec calendar**, the original of which can be found in the National Museum of Anthropology in Mexico City.

Imagine That!

Feel at home in La Hacienda? Probably because it is designed to represent a Mexican hacienda, hence the restaurant's name, which means "the home." General Manager Darwin Bravo explains: "The main dining room represents the home's dining room, the room with blue lights is the living room, the small room designed with stone is the home's pantry, and the room with star-shaped light fixtures is the banquet room, where the family would throw lavish parties."

Gran Fiesta Tour Starring the Three Caballeros

Before you enter the queue for the attraction, pause for a few minutes and watch the volcano scene just across the River of Time. Every now and then **the volcano erupts**.

That **googly-eyed head** you pass when you enter the first scene after the tunnel is a replica of an actual stone carving in the National Museum of Anthropology in Mexico City.

Apparently Donald has passed this way before. During the Day of the Dead celebration you'll see children whacking a **Donald-shaped piñata**.

China

The China pavilion's Temple of Heaven, a true half-scale representation of the Beijing Temple, is filled with symbolism. The real Temple of Heaven in China is a complex, and the Hall of Prayer for Good Harvest is the central, circular building.

Built as a place of prayer for a successful harvest, each element has meaning, with a surprising secret in the heart of the temple.

It's easy to overlook the writing you see all around World Showcase when it's in a foreign language. But don't. Some interesting things are being expressed. Notice the writing on the Zhao Yang Men, **Gate of the Golden Sun**, at the entry to the pavilion. It's Mandarin for "Going toward the sun gate," but its meaning is more than simply moving toward the sun. It really means something akin to "moving into daylight and basking in the beauty of the sun."

Now take a look at the left side of the gift shop next to the Joy of Tea kiosk. The Mandarin lettering reads **Good Fortune**, which is a nice sentiment, but also appropriate since it's the name of the shop.

Look at the floor as you walk through the temple's front doors. The **concentric circles** move inward in multiples of three (three symbolizing living or giving life, and also the trinity of heaven, earth, and man in Chinese numerology) until they reach the center circle. Stand with your feet directly over the circle and say something, anything. The building is acoustically perfect, causing your voice to vibrate directly back into your ears. Step outside the circle, even just one step, and speak again. Notice the difference? You can whisper as you stand over the circle and still have the effect of hearing your voice as it bounces back to you. Notice how it sounds slightly different from the way you hear it inside your head.

Looking progressively upward, the temple's **four columns** represent the four seasons, the **twelve pillars** are representative of the twelve months of the Chinese year, and the **twelve outer pillars** are the twelve-hour division of day and of night. Combine the two sets of pillars and you have a representation of **one solar term**.

As you stand under the domed roof look for key symbols in the elaborate design. **Pairings of nine** in Chinese cosmology represent the heart, heaven, and the eight directions plus the center. **Earth** is represented by squares, while **heaven** is represented by round elements. The building's **three stories** signify heaven, earth, and humans. **Blue** indicates heaven, **yellow** indicates earth, and **green** signifies mortality and the mortal world.

Imagine That!

Ron Rodriguez, Director of Talent Casting and Booking for Walt Disney Creative Entertainment, talks about casting the original performers when Epcot opened: "The performers in the China pavilion auditioned in Orlando, and only one of them, David Chen, was actually Chinese. He played the Chinese flute, and spoke no English. What were we going to do? Eight months later we brought in a girl who did ribbon dancing, and we put her with the flute. Dave was washing windows at a hotel, and was the producer of his own company, Dragon Legend Entertainment. We flew him to China and he came back with a huge group of entertainers. Dave went to mayors in China for visas rather than the central government, which was a much more successful route."

Two recurring themes are the **phoenix and the dragon**, representing the empress and the emperor, respectively. Notice some dragons have only four fingers. They represent masculinity in general; in a spiritual context, such as here in the temple, they are the generators of wind and rain, aptly placed in a temple of prayer for abundant crops. Only the five-fingered dragon represents the emperor.

As you tour the pavilion you'll notice more writing on some of the columns outside the shops and homes. During festivals or other special occasions, shop and home owners in China adorn their columns with **quotes from poets** or with **wishes for health or prosperity**. When writing is seen on temple columns, it indicates a prayer. The owner of the first shop you reach on the right-hand side is covering all the bases. The writing on the column on the left is a request for greater income year by year and the writing on the column on the right is a wish for good luck.

Enter the House of Good Fortune and look down at the floor. The design mimics a **bridge over a lotus pond**, and if you listen closely you'll hear birdsong. Wealthier homeowners use the real thing as a decorative technique to induce a sense of relaxation and well-being.

Just to the right of the House of Good Fortune is a small general store that is "owned" by the private company that sponsors the China pavilion. The upper apartment features a balcony with a **cherry blossom tree**, symbolic to the Japanese of the beauty and fragility of life.

Fascinating Fact

Dragons can be found in male and female form, though only male dragons are depicted in Epcot's China pavilion. How are female dragons identified? They have fans on their tail instead of a club, the spikes on their mane are rounded on the ends, their snout is straight, and their horns are thicker at the base than at the tips. Next time you encounter a dragon you'll know whether you're facing a male or a female, but rest assured, unlike their Japanese cousins, Chinese dragons are benevolent . . . unless you anger them!

At the end of each ornate upward-tilting roofline, you will see a small character on the back of a chicken (yes, it's a chicken!). That's evil **King Min of the state of Qi**, ruler of China, who was hung from his ancestral temple's rooftop in 284 B.C.E. at the command of the prime minister.

Superstition dictates that a representation of King Min sitting on the roof will protect that building from evil spirits. As added insurance, he is guarded by helpful animals that line up behind him keeping watch. The number of animals guarding King Min indicates the status of that particular building.

Outpost

After you leave China, take a short diversion into the Africa-themed Outpost, just across the bridge. The humble little Outpost doesn't have a lot to offer beyond snacks and drinks, but you'll still find a bit of hidden magic here. Coca-Cola is being shipped in from around the world, as evidenced by **various languages on the crates and coolers**. Along with Korean and Russian, look for the Chinese markings on a red cooler which, loosely translated, mean "let me treat you to a drink." The Arabic words on a large gray crate at the left of the pavilion simply read, "Drink Coca-Cola."

Germany

As you stroll from pavilion to pavilion, each one captures your imagination in a different way. Many visitors feel Germany in particular has something just a bit special about it. The theme here feels familiar and homey, perhaps due to all those Brothers Grimm fairy tales we heard as children, many of which have their roots in Germanic folk stories.

If you've ever visited Germany and recall that there are four **Habsburg princes** on the façade of the Kaufhaus in Freiburg (on which Epcot's Das Kaufhaus is based), you'd be correct. Why are there only three here? Because there wasn't room to place all four of them on the ledge and still maintain the illusion of size through forced perspective, so only Philip I, Charles V, and Ferdinand I made the final cut. Maximilian I is the missing prince.

The painting on the wall opposite the Sommerfest quick-service dining location is designed to look like a tapestry featuring the famous **Rothenburg ob der Tauber**, considered one of Germany's most romantically styled villages. In reality, the painting covers what would have been the entry to a never-built Rhine River cruise attraction intended for the pavilion.

The crests you see on the front of Das Kaufhaus are re-creations of the Imperial German Eagle and a crown. Eagles with one head represent the **German Empire** from 1871 through 1918, and those with two heads represent the **Holy Roman Empire**. One head represents the church and the other represents the state.

Italy

Much of the Italy pavilion is based on the timeless city of Venice, with a nearly exact replica of **Saint Mark's Square**, but in mirror image. Why is the square backward?

Because the blueprints Disney was using were taken from a photograph that was transposed when it was developed.

Here you'll find a hidden gem that has the kind of creepy backstory I just love. Walk to the end of the pink Doge's Palace and turn left. See that **face on the wall** with its mouth wide open? It isn't just a decorative element. Faces like this one were akin to mail slots, through which the good townspeople were encouraged to slip notes reporting the transgressions of their neighbors. The catch was, you had to sign the paper so everyone knew who was doing the snitching. If you didn't sign it, your complaint was considered nothing but gossip.

The Doge's Palace is beautiful indeed, but the palace in Venice also has a darker side. Deep inside the palace ways **a prison and torture chamber**, where enemies of the state endured interrogation. The famous lover Casanova was incarcerated there until his escape to Paris in 1756.

With that in mind, notice the bridge on the second story at the back of the Doge's Palace. It represents the infamous **Bridge of Sighs** that convicts would have crossed on their way to the palace's prison. Those who entered had little hope for survival, hence the bridge's sorrowful name.

Imagine That!

Imagineer Ron Rodriguez remembers the challenges of booking the original entertainment for the Italy pavilion: "Sonny Anderson, then the Director of Casting and Booking in California, was traveling in Italy and sent me some entertainers to rehearse for the Alfredo restaurant in the Italy pavilion in Epcot. None of them spoke English. They were opera singers, and while there were some tough times communicating, they finally got it and turned it into a great show."

Turn around and walk to the right side of the pavilion, where you'll find a door with columns on either side. What is the meaning of this passageway to nowhere? The columns represent the **classical orders**, three distinct styles that show the progression of column architecture over the years. Starting with the earliest style at the bottom of the left-hand column, they run from Doric used by the Greeks and Romans, to Ionic, which became popular in 570 B.C.E., to Corinthian, which appeared in 450 B.C.E. All are styles still used today, though Corinthian's ornate style remains the most popular.

Pop into Via Napoli for a quick look at their **wood-burning pizza ovens**, or better yet, have a meal there. The faces that frame the ovens are the mythological goddess Etna, who lends her name to an active volcano in Sicily; volcano Vesuvius in Naples, which honors the demigod Hercules; and Stromboli, volcanic home to Aeolus, keeper of the wind. Notice, however, that all three faces are male, but Etna is, in mythology, a female. Why does she have the characteristics of a male? Because the images were taken from ancient tile work in Rome.

Fascinating Fact

How is Vesuvius linked to Hercules? Hercules is the son of Zeus, whose nickname is sometimes recorded as Ves. The Greek name Vesouuios translates as "son of Ves," and its pronunciation was corrupted to Vesuvius.

The water fountain at the far-right side of the Italy pavilion as you walk toward the American Adventure features a pretty tile-work slogan. What does **Alla Salute** mean? "To your health!"

The American Adventure

Welcome, one and all, to the United States of America! Situated as the central pavilion in World Showcase, the American Adventure plays host to all the countries surrounding her, spreading her architectural arms wide in a gesture of hospitality. The spaciousness afforded to the pavilion and inclusion of the America Gardens Theater serve to highlight Walt Disney's pride in his country and his desire to share her bounty with all nations.

The building's architecture and the round-top doorway into the pavilion are **Georgian**, a style widely employed from the years 1700 to 1780, and the square doors leading into the rotunda are **Federal**, which gained popularity from 1780 to 1820. The dates are a clue to why the Georgian construction, so named for the kings of England, fell out of favor and the Federal theme surged; the American Revolutionary War to gain independence from England ended in 1783.

The American Adventure building was constructed from 110,000 handmade **Georgia clay bricks**, which were designed to look old in keeping with the pavilion's time frame.

The **American eagle** on top of the attraction's sign plays a key role in the nation's psyche. Here, he's looking to the left, toward the olive branch grasped in his claw, widely considered an indication that the nation is at peace. Before you enter the rotunda notice the direction the eagle above the door is facing. While he is still facing the olive branch, his head is now pointing to the right.

Fascinating Fact

The original left-facing eagle is "militarily incorrect." This head placement changed in 1945 under President Harry Truman's administration, inspired by President Roosevelt's petition to correct a discrepancy between the number of stars on the flag of the commander in chief and the number of stars generals or fleet admirals in World War II were given. When the military status of five-star was added, President Roosevelt felt the four stars on the commander in chief flag were inadequate. It was during this transition that heraldic expert Arthur E. DuBois noticed the eagle's incorrect head placement, and since 1949 the eagle faces right, a direction customarily indicating honor, regardless of the nation being at war or at peace.

The windows on either side of the front entry feature busts of **Mark Twain** (on the right) and **Benjamin Franklin** (on the left), hosts of the pavilion's attraction. Models of statues that flank either side of the American Adventure stage can also be seen. These are casts of the models used by Disney Legend Blaine Gibson when creating the statues and Audio-Animatronic faces of Franklin and Twain for the show.

Before you head into the rotunda for the fabulous Voices of Liberty a capella group or to see the American Adventure show, take a moment to look at two sets of **silhouettes in the lobby**. Turn left just after you enter and you'll see one set on the wall to your left, featuring two script writers for the American Adventure. On the same wall but to the right of the doorway are two more silhouettes. The gentleman is one of the pavilion's head architects and the woman is a head interior designer.

Fascinating Fact

There was a time when architecture was filled with symbolism. Even walls told a story, beginning at the floor, which was symbolic of the earth, the ground, and chaos. As the eye traveled up the wall, chaos was replaced by order. The system was incredibly complex, full of mystic references to gods, ritual sacrifice, life, and death. While the meanings of these molding details have largely been lost or corrupted, it isn't difficult to get the general idea if you take the time to look.

The frieze that runs just below the ceiling in the lobby holds a symbolic secret. The **bowl and garland** represent the blending of cultures that made the United States a true melting pot, with the bowl representing other nations and the garland being the ribbon tying them together. The classic **egg-and-dart crown molding** above the bowls was used during colonial times to indicate a family member was born, lived, and died in the same house. Eggs were representative of birth, life, and the universe, but they were also used in ritual sacrifices as food for the gods.

In Greek mythology, Aphrodite gave a rose to her son Eros, which he then gave to Harpocrates, the god of silence, to ensure secrecy regarding Aphrodite's romantic indiscretions. The **rose detailing** recalls this tale, and has become a symbol of confidentiality.

Dentiles (the trim that looks like a string of boxes with gaps between them) represent ornamental teeth, symbolic of eating, which is necessary for life. Who knew architecture could tell such elaborate stories?

As you are watching the American Adventure show, take note of Mr. Brady, the photographer in the Americans Divided scene. He is meant to be **Mathew Brady**, famed Civil War photographer.

The **"Two Brothers"** song in American Adventure is the folk song "Two Brothers (One Blue, One Gray)," written by Irving Gordon in 1951. In the original version, a second verse speaks of two sisters in black waiting by the train tracks for their sweethearts to come back.

The **gas station scene** is beautifully evocative of the era, and for a good reason. It is based heavily on a photograph taken by renowned photographer Dorothea Lange in 1936. Lange specialized in photographing migrant and homeless people during the Great Depression, and may be most famous for her portrait *Migrant Mother*.

Once you've seen the American Adventure show you'll be singing the ending song, "Golden Dream," in your head for days. And then, just when you've forgotten about it, you'll see the ship in the harbor behind the America Gardens Theater and it will all come flooding back. Why? Because the name on the back of this Virginia sloop replica is **Golden Dream**, in honor of the song.

Imagine That!

As Manager of Entertainment Staffing, Gene Columbus knew how to create the kind of special events Disney does so well. But there was one event that stands out for him: "There are so many special events and productions to be proud of, but the one that sticks out in my mind was the twenty-fifth anniversary of Special Olympics. We kept adjusting the scope of the event so Disney could provide more experiences to the families attending the event, and as the producer I had to keep adjusting and working with my operational partners to find ways to reduce costs. Everyone worked hard to make it happen and I am sure many of those people share how proud they are for pulling this event off in such a grand scale with a small budget. As part of the program there was a drawing to select the Special Olympian to carry the torch to light the cauldron on stage, and this was done only hours before the big celebration. When the young man arrived at America Gardens stage in Epcot he was in a wheelchair, and as I briefed him he was very clear that he would not use his chair but would walk to the stage carrying the torch. I was so taken with this young man and his determination, and when that moment came he proudly stood up and began walking toward the stage. The audience jumped to their feet and you could see the joint emotion of the young man and this large audience. About halfway, it became apparent that he was having difficulties and was not going to make it, but his father came out of nowhere and grabbed his son before he fell and helped him to the stage. He did not take the torch as his son continued on his quest to light the cauldron. The moment the flame burned brightly the young man turned to the audience, with his father stepping backward to ensure the glory was for his son, and the brilliance of this young man's smile and pride shined as brightly as the flame. I admit that tears were rolling down my cheek and each time I see the America Garden stage I have a flash of that very magical moment."

Japan

Arriving in Japan, the main building sets a graceful tone. Warm wood and clean, flowing lines combine simplicity with timeless beauty, and as you would expect, there is a great deal of symbolism present.

The garden you see at the front of the pavilion is a **Japanese dry garden**. Rocks placed in the dry garden traditionally represent ships or islands while the gravel serves as the sea.

One of the key concepts in a proper Japanese stone garden is the arrangement of elements in odd numbers, and the most important arrangement of stones is that of the *sanson*, or **the three Buddha**. Look for the three rocks on the extreme right side of the small rock garden as you are facing Mitsukoshi. The large stone in the middle of this pairing represents the Buddha and the two accompanying stones represent bodhisattvas, individuals who have achieved enlightenment but delay their journey to nirvana so that they may assist others who are suffering or in need of compassion. Bodhisattvas also represent the past lives of the Buddha.

As you walk toward Mitsukoshi, take a look at the **stone lantern** in the landscaping in front of the store, on the right-hand side. It was given to Roy O. Disney by the Japanese government to honor the opening of the Japan pavilion in 1982.

Here's another foreign-language reading lesson: The letters above the fortress in Japan are a friendly greeting which reads **konnichiha** (pronounced: koh-nee-chee-wah), the Japanese word meaning "hello."

The **golden fish** on the blue roof above the fortress at the back of the pavilion is one of Buddhism's eight auspicious symbols. It is a reminder to live in a state of fearlessness, moving freely through life. Just as fish do not fear drowning, humans should not fear drowning in their suffering.

Morocco

Morocco is one of Epcot's most beautiful pavilions, full of vibrant colors and startling patterns. It was important to the sponsors that traditional artistic customs be honored; hence they used their own artists to create the thousands of tiles and carvings you see.

Spice Road Table was added to the Morocco pavilion in 2013, with plenty of symbolism if you know what to look for. The blue paint in and on the building represents **Morocco's coastal cities**, while the windows in the indoor dining room represent **Portuguese control** and the influence it had on Moroccan architecture. The dining-room **chandeliers** are all different in honor of Morocco's diversity. The tower outside looks like the south of Morocco, and the rest of the exterior looks like the north. The south is represented by the color red and the north by white, blue, and green. And, of course, its location on the waterfront is symbolic of Morocco's borders along the Mediterranean Sea and the Atlantic Ocean.

Imagine That!

Spice Road Table's Executive Chef, Samad Benzari, was born in Morocco and has a fond appreciation for Spice Road Table's authenticity. He says, "Artists came from Morocco and created the restaurant's interior. The copper tables are carved by hand and came directly from Morocco. Even the tiles on the bar came from Morocco. The only things we got from here are the plates, spoons, and glasses."

Pay close attention to the architecture of the pavilion. If you start at the back, it takes you from ancient history to more modern-day building styles, as would be typical in Moroccan cities. The architecture toward the back is representative of a castle around which the city would have grown, becoming progressively more modern farther from the castle.

You'll know you've reached the **Fez House** when you enter the small courtyard decorated almost entirely in tiles. The upper story is the homeowner's living quarters. If you stop and listen, you'll hear the family inside (wait for it!). Apparently a guest has shown up unannounced and the family is bustling about to get refreshments. If you pay close attention, you may hear the tea service hit the floor when one of the children trips over another in his haste to set out a snack. Stand there long enough and you'll hear the English-speaking guest arrive.

You may recall the Cast Member signature book in Journey into Imagination with Figment, and you'll find a lovely version of this sentimental memorial here in Morocco. On the wall just inside the second door to the right of the entry to the Tangier Traders shop, you'll see a **pretty wooden board** that looks like a work of art. Moroccan Cast Members doing their international internship program at Epcot sign their names in Arabic, and this is just one of several boards that have been filled with signatures since the pavilion opened.

Remember your reading lessons from Africa, China, and Japan? Let's look at another one in Morocco. The Arabic carving that tops the replica of the Nejjarine Fountain forms the words *Aliiz Lillah*, or "All greatness, all mystery, all power of the Creator."

Stand near the Nejjarine Fountain for a few minutes and you may hear a **conversation from within the shop** behind you. The merchant and one of his patrons are discussing some of the shop's items.

On the opposite side of the courtyard you'll hear other sounds of everyday life. Particularly enchanting are the **singing children**, happily chiming out a song about their school life and lessons, just as they do in real-life Morocco.

France

Imagineers strive to create realistic settings, remaining true to the experience you would have when traveling abroad. Usually the inspiration is taken from real life. That is certainly the case here in the France pavilion.

See that unusual **petal-shaped glass covering** over the arcade to the left of Plume et Pallete? It's a re-creation of the Porte Dauphine station entryway of the Paris Métro. The original archway was designed by Hector Guimard, widely considered to be France's most important art nouveau architect.

Les Halles (pronounced "ley-al"), at the back of the pavilion, features some of the most appealing quick-bite offerings in all of World Showcase. The counter service section is based on the **Parisian fresh-food market** of the same name, while the exterior, the seating area, and the gift shop are designed to look like a typical **French train station**.

This may not be hidden magic as much as an almost-hidden oops! As you are watching *Impressions de France*, look quickly to the extreme right-hand screen when the Vézelay Abbey scene ends and the church bells finish chiming. The movie's editors didn't notice the **reflection of the cameraman and the camera trolley** in the shop window, but now that you know what to look for, you'll notice it!

While it makes for a convenient pathway from France to the United Kingdom pavilion, the bridge you cross is based on the real-life pedestrian bridge **Pont des Arts**, which links the Louvre and Institut de France, crossing the River Seine. Don't forget to look over each side of the bridge as you make your crossing.

United Kingdom

British visitors may feel they have returned home when they reach the United Kingdom pavilion. At least, they would if they lived at **Hampton Court**, the palace that inspired the building housing the Toy Soldier shop and the Sportsman's Shoppe, across from the Rose & Crown Pub.

The **coat of arms** above the Sportsman's Shoppe's High Street entry is loosely based on the royal arms used from the time of King Henry VI through the reign of Queen Elizabeth I. The authentic crest features three lions in the upper right and lower left quadrants, and three French fleur-de-lis in the upper left and lower right quadrants. Epcot's crest is an example of how Imagineers sometimes use a real-life item or concept and blur the lines, so to speak, when they choose not to create an exact reproduction.

The façade of the Sportsman's Shoppe is based on a small section of Scottish author Sir Walter Scott's **Abbotsford**

House, with short twin towers next to the entry, and small upper turrets.

The U.K. pavilion is a mix of historical times and locations, primarily representing pre-1949 Britain. How do we know this? Besides the obvious time frames depicted by the buildings, there are several references to Britain before Ireland gained full independence from the Commonwealth. Inside the Crown and Crest you'll find a coat of arms on the wall featuring **icons representing England, Scotland, Ireland, and Wales**. You'll also find Irish merchandise in the shops and Guinness beer in the pub, though only Northern Ireland is still part of the United Kingdom.

A standout feature of the Crown and Crest shop is the **carved wooden door frame** depicting a knight on one side and a priest on the other. Carved door frames were a sign of wealth and the number of elaborate rosettes, horns of plenty, and heavenly hosts indicate this homeowner was well-off indeed.

Before you pop in to the Queen's Table, notice the crests in the shop's upstairs window. They represent **Oxford, Eton, Edinburgh, and Cambridge**, four of the United Kingdom's historic seats of learning.

As you walk out of the pavilion, take a look at the three stained-glass windows to the left of the **Crown and Crest sign**, representing each of the three flags (England, Scotland, and Wales) that make up the Union Jack. Their mottos are **Tria juncta in uno** (Wales: "three joined in one," motto of the Order of the Bath); **Nemo me impune lacessit** (Scotland: "nobody assails me with impunity," motto of Scotland and the Order of the Thistle); and **Honi soit qui mal y pense** (England: "evil be to him who evil thinks," motto of the Order of the Garter).

Rose and Crown's motto, posted above the doorway to the restaurant, reads **Otium cum dignitate**. Translated it means "leisure with dignity," a mighty fine way to conduct oneself through life. However, it may be worth noting at the time the phrase was coined, those who were able to afford leisure also associated the perk with another possible definition of the word *dignity*, which is "worthiness." The upper classes were considered worthy of leisure, with dignity or not.

Fascinating Fact

The Order of the Garter's origins are unclear, but a charming possibility lies in the mishap of the Countess of Salisbury, whose garter slipped from her leg while she was dancing in the company of King Edward. Unkind laughter on the part of various courtiers nearby prompted the king to utter the phrase, "Shamed be the person who thinks evil of it," that would inspire the order's motto.

The Rose and Crown Pub and Yorkshire County Fish Shop each have an obvious purpose, but what is that little building in between? In reality, it's a Cast Member area. In the story, it's a lockkeeper's home. Walk down the path behind the house and the fish and chip shop, and look for a sign on the back of the building. It reads, **Grand Union Canal, Thomas Dudley, Lockkeeper**. England's Grand Union Canal spans 137 miles between Birmingham and London and features 166 locks. Walk down to the waterfront and you'll see the United Kingdom pavilion's version of the canal.

Canada

Arriving at the final pavilion on our clockwise tour, **two distinct styles** become obvious. Eastern Canada is represented by the brick structures, while wood was the building material of choice in western Canada. The history of Canada, from the early European trappers to the nineteenth-century Victorian influence, blends seamlessly, while the impressive Butchart-inspired sunken garden brings a grace and beauty to the otherwise rough terrain of the Canadian Rocky Mountains.

The pavilion expresses Canada's diversity, from the obvious **Canadian Rockies** to the waterfall representing **Salmon Falls** in New Brunswick, totem poles symbolic of the **Northwest coast**, and the country's capital of **Ottawa**, reflected in the hotel, which is based in part on Chateau Laurier.

Imagine That!

Being in a position of authority comes with its challenges, especially when an issue is personal. Ron Rodriguez recalls, "When Disney brought in BeeBee La Crème, a French Canadian jazz accordion player for the Canada pavilion, he had a big beard. I was the one who had to tell him he had to shave it off to conform to Disney standards of the time. The next day he came in with a plastic container with his beard in it and gave it to me."

Canadian hotels Chateau Frontenac in Quebec City, Chateau Laurier in Ottawa, and Fairmont Banff Springs in Alberta were the inspiration for **Hotel du Canada**, but there is a tragic historical tie-up here, too. Chateau Laurier was commissioned by American railroader Charles Melville Hays, who never saw the opening of the hotel. He perished just days prior to the opening while making the return trip to Ottawa from England onboard the RMS *Titanic*.

Only one of the **totem poles** in the Canada pavilion is real. Can you tell which one? (See Solution 3 in Appendix: Solutions to Hints for the answer.) The real totem pole was commissioned by Walt Disney Imagineering, who realized the error of their creative ways when they placed the totem pole crafted by a native artist next to the one Imagineering had already created and saw how cartoonlike theirs looked in comparison.

Alaskan artist David Boxley's totem pole depicts a traditional **Raven story**, one of many told by the Tsimshian people as well as other Pacific Northwest indigenous peoples. Raven is a trickster whose antics often backfire, but everything somehow comes out right in the end, with a generous helping of insight into the customs of the Northwest natives' way of life. Here, Raven is forcing the Chief of the Skies to release the sun, the moon, and the stars.

Imagine That!

What is it like to design stage sets for something as beloved as Epcot's seasonal show *Candlelight Processional*? Cindy White says, "It is an honor, plain and simple. The director of the 2012 show, Forrest Bahruth, was the most experienced director on property, truly a treasure to work with, and the perfect creative vision for taking this classic presentation and giving it the upgrade and refresh it deserved. I got to art direct Forrest's vision of creating modern vibrant stained-glass windows with a star motif, creating a new overhead star. Most importantly, he wanted to get the entire tree riser back into a traditional pyramidal shape, which is no easy task on the low-rise America Gardens stage. There are singing Christmas tree choirs in large churches all over America and beyond, but at Walt Disney World it needed elegance— hence the addition of a gilt tracery balustrade—and safety above and beyond any choral riser out there."

And if you think you've seen everything just by touring the park, there's one more spectacle most people miss at Epcot.

As the crowds rush to the exit after IllumiNations ends, slow your pace and let World Showcase empty out. Now is the perfect time to stroll the walkway amid the peacefulness and the twinkling lights, and there is one final act that has to play out before Epcot is put to bed for the night. At some point between 10:00 and 10:30, the inferno barge out on World Showcase Lagoon undergoes a **fuel burn-off**, which, if you didn't know better, looks like the barge is exploding. It's an astonishing (but quick) sight and if you have the stamina to stick around for it, it's something you won't soon forget.

Discovery is Epcot's primary focus. Take the time to wander. You may just find that "one little spark" of imagination that inspired Epcot's opening-day theme, "We've Just Begun to Dream!"

Epcot Timeline

Walt Disney first described plans for Epcot, the Experimental Prototype Community of Tomorrow, in October 1966, envisioning a working city where technology and creativity would combine, showcasing American ingenuity and the concept of free enterprise. He never saw his dream realized, because Walt passed away on December 15, 1966.

The park opened on October 1, 1982. During the opening-day ceremonies, Card Walker greeted guests with what is now a quintessential Disney slogan: "To all who enter this place of Joy, Hope, and Friendship—Welcome."

1982: Opening Attractions
The park opened with a series of special dedication ceremonies for the various attractions. The ceremonies took

place during the first few weeks of the park's existence and highlighted each of the main attractions in turn.

Spaceship Earth was dedicated on October 1, 1982, followed by the **China** pavilion on the third, **Universe of Energy** on the fourth, **World of Motion** on the fifth, **the Land** on the sixth, **the American Adventure** on the eleventh and twelfth, **Canada** on the thirteenth, **Italy** on the fourteenth, **Germany** on the fifteenth, **Communicore** on the eighteenth, **United Kingdom** on the nineteenth, and **France** and **Japan** on the twentieth.

The official **grand opening** took place October 22–24, 1982, with a dedication ceremony on the twenty-fourth. Representatives from around the world participated in a water-pouring ceremony, adding water from major rivers and seas around the world to the fountain in Innoventions Plaza. On October 23, Epcot's first nighttime fireworks show, **Carnival de Lumiere**, began.

On December 4, 1982, **Journey into Imagination** was dedicated, followed by **Mexico** on December 13.

1983–1988: A Period of IllumiNation

Horizons opened on October 1, 1983, with **New World Fantasy** replacing Carnival de Lumiere as the evening fireworks spectacle. On June 9, 1984, Epcot hosted World Fest, featuring its first lagoon-based fireworks show, **Laserphonic Fantasy**. **Morocco** followed on September 7, 1984, the tenth pavilion in World Showcase.

Daytime show **Skyleidoscope** air and water pageant debuted in 1985, along with China's **Nine Dragons Restaurant** and **Lotus Blossom Café**, but it would take until January 15, 1986, for another major attraction, **The**

Living Seas, to open its doors, adding an eighth significant element to Future World.

The ground-breaking **Captain EO**, a blockbuster 3D film produced by George Lucas, directed by Francis Ford Coppola, and starring pop singer Michael Jackson, debuted on September 12, 1986, at the Magic Eye Theater, located in the same building as Journey into Imagination.

Two years later, on January 30, 1988, the breathtaking **IllumiNations** nighttime laser and fireworks show premiered, replacing Laserphonic Fantasy. Then, on May 6, 1988, World Showcase welcomed the **Norway** pavilion, with the pavilion's ride, **Maelstrom**, opening four days later.

1989–1994: Wonders, Surprises, and Innoventions

On October 19, 1989, the **Wonders of Life** pavilion opened in Future World, and Walt Disney World celebrated its twentieth anniversary a year later, an occasion honored at Epcot by the arrival of **Surprise in the Skies** daytime show over the World Showcase Lagoon.

Another three years would pass before any major changes occurred, including an alteration to the park's name, as EPCOT Center officially became **Epcot '94**. On March 26, **Food Rocks** replaced Kitchen Kabaret at the Land pavilion, while Communicore closed in January, returning as **Innoventions East and West** on July 1, and the very first **Flower and Garden Festival** was held—now one of the park's most successful annual events.

Next up was **Honey, I Shrunk the Audience**, a 3D experience based on the hit movie *Honey, I Shrunk the Kids*, which arrived at the Magic Eye Theater on November 21, replacing *Captain EO*.

1995–1998: New Years, New Names

With the New Year came (another) new name, **Epcot '95**. Also new, on January 21, 1995, *Circle of Life: An Environmental Fable* replaced *Symbiosis* at the Land pavilion. The show featured characters from the blockbuster motion picture *The Lion King*; Disney movies had begun to play a role in Epcot's attractions. That summer, the first **Food and Wine Festival** debuted, another popular annual event that has gone on to become a major money-spinner.

Again, as the year changed so did the park's name, this time simply shortened (thankfully) to **Epcot**. World of Motion pavilion closed on January 2, 1996, in preparation for a new attraction that would be so technologically advanced, its original projected opening date of summer 1997 was delayed for nearly two years as Imagineers worked out the bugs.

Ellen's Energy Adventure, starring popular television personalities Ellen DeGeneres and Bill Nye, replaced the original Universe of Energy show on September 15, 1996, adding a lighter touch to an attraction that was considered by some to be "too dry and factual."

1999–2000: Millennium Milestones

After a sixteen-year run, the Horizons pavilion closed on January 9, 1999, and finally, on March 7, **Test Track** made its long-awaited debut in the former World of Motion pavilion, racing its way into Epcot history as the attraction with the worst track record for breakdowns. However, the ride also became wildly popular, in contrast to **Journey into Your Imagination**, which effectively killed off beloved characters Dreamfinder and Figment when it replaced Journey into Imagination on October 1, 1999.

Unveiled on September 29, 1999, the massive **Mickey Wand** towered alongside Spaceship Earth, with its glittering Epcot 2000 signage. It would remain there for seven years, minus the 2000 portion once the Millennium Celebration ended.

The year-long celebration also scored a huge hit with the **Tapestry of Nations** parade and the specially revamped **IllumiNations: Reflections of Earth** laser and fireworks show, which debuted along with Journey into Your Imagination. Tapestry of Nations would be renamed **Tapestry of Dreams** in 2000, before ending its run in March 2003.

2001–2004: Figment Returns!

With a nod toward the public outcry caused by the original attraction's closure, **Journey into Imagination with Figment** replaced the 1999 version on June 1, 2002, and, happily, resurrected the little purple dragon.

Reflections of China replaced Circle-Vision 360° *Wonders of China* on May 22, 2003, and another three months would pass before the state-of-the-art ride **Mission: SPACE** debuted on August 15, undergoing various adjustments over the course of the next few years as guests suffered motion sickness due to the realistic sensation of launching into space provided by the ride system's centrifuge.

Food Rocks at the Land pavilion closed in January 2004, making room for a new attraction due the following year. At the Living Seas, the hugely imaginative **Turtle Talk with Crush** debuted in November 2004, adding more entertainment geared toward the six and under crowd, bringing another megahit movie character (from *Finding Nemo*) to Epcot—and creating far bigger crowds than anyone imagined!

2005–2006: The Land Has Liftoff

On May 5, 2005, Disneyland import **Soarin'** opened at the Land pavilion, housed in a brand-new building branching off the main pavilion. A direct copy of Soarin' over California from Disney's California Adventure park, the attraction was an immediate success, with waiting time frequently topping 180 minutes.

Riding a tidal wave of popularity caused by Turtle Talk with Crush, the Living Seas underwent a much-needed refurbishment and emerged with a new name, **the Seas with Nemo & Friends**, in October 2006.

2007: Twenty-Five Years to Celebrate

El Rio del Tiempo in the Mexico pavilion went down for refurbishment and returned on April 6 as the **Gran Fiesta Tour Starring the Three Caballeros**. The park's icon, Spaceship Earth, also closed for a major overhaul shortly after its post-show area reopened after several years of dormancy as **Project Tomorrow: Inventing the Wonders of the Future**.

In another long-overdue move, the Circle-Vision 360° film *O Canada!* returned on September 1, redone with comedian Martin Short as its onscreen host.

October 1, 2007, marked Epcot's twenty-fifth anniversary. Though no formal celebrations had been announced by Disney, a dedicated fan base organized a grassroots acknowledgment of the milestone called **Celebration 25**. Epcot's vice president, Jim MacPhee, announced a rededication ceremony would take place, highlighted by a second water-pouring ceremony and "A Conversation with Marty Sklar," during which Disney Legend Sklar spoke about the creation of the park, the challenges the Imagineers faced, and the impact Walt

Disney's grand vision, realized in part through Epcot, has had upon the world.

2008–2014: A Time of Rediscovery

The years 2008 through 2014 were a time of shifting and changing rather than grand debuts. **Honey, I Shrunk the Audience** closed May 9, 2010, to make way for the reopening of *Captain EO* on July 2, 2010.

Test Track closed on April 15, 2012, reopening on December 6, 2012, with a new theme and with Chevrolet as its sponsor.

World Showcase Players had their last performance September 25, 2014, while hugely popular musical groups **Off Kilter**, **Spirit of America Fife and Drum Corps**, and **Mo'Rockin'** each had their final performances on September 27, 2014, to make way for new entertainment. The **Canadian Lumberjacks** show began performances on October 6, 2014, at the Mill Stage next to the Canada pavilion; flag-waving performers **Sbandieratori di Sansepolcro** began on October 19 in Italy; **the Paul McKenna Band** brought Celtic folk music to the United Kingdom on November 26, and folk music and dancers **B'net Al Houwariyate** began performing at Morocco on November 2.

Fan favorite **Maelstrom** closed October 6, 2014, and the Norway pavilion was rethemed to Disney's movie *Frozen*.

Hollywood Studios

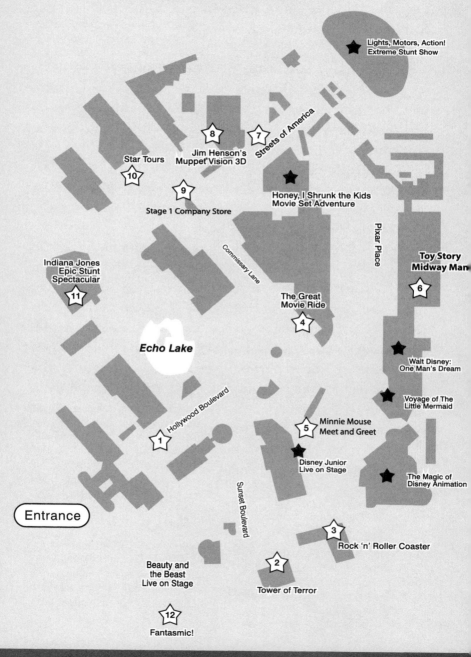

Lights, Motors, Action!
Extreme Stunt Show

Streets of America

Jim Henson's
Muppet Vision 3D

Star Tours

Honey, I Shrunk the Kids
Movie Set Adventure

Stage 1 Company Store

Pixar Place

Toy Story
Midway Man

Indiana Jones
Epic Stunt
Spectacular

The Great
Movie Ride

Walt Disney:
One Man's Dream

Echo Lake

Voyage of The
Little Mermaid

Minnie Mouse
Meet and Greet

Hollywood Boulevard

Disney Junior
Live on Stage

The Magic of
Disney Animation

Entrance

Sunset Boulevard

Rock 'n' Roller Coaster

Beauty and
the Beast
Live on Stage

Tower of Terror

Fantasmic!

1. **Hollywood Boulevard:** The half-oval plate in the pavement at the junction of Hollywood Boulevard and Sunset Boulevard is marked Est. 1928, the year Mickey Mouse was first featured in the cartoon short *Steamboat Willie*.

2. **Tower of Terror:** Inside each elevator is a safety inspection certificate signed by Mr. Cadwallader and dated October 31, 1939, the day the Tower Hotel opened. The inspection certificate is number 10259, the numeric version of October 2, 1959, and refers to the date the first *Twilight Zone* episode aired.

3. **Rock 'n' Roller Coaster:** The delivery address for G-Force Records reads 1401 Flower Street. Why did Imagineers choose that street and number? It's the address of Walt Disney Imagineering in Glendale, California.

4. **The Great Movie Ride:** In the James Cagney scene just after the Mary Poppins setting, the bottom of one of the posters on the wall has been torn, and you can see Mickey Mouse's shoes peeking out from behind.

5. **Minnie Mouse Meet and Greet:** The *Ailurophobia* movie poster in the queue for Minnie Mouse's meet-and-greet refers to the fear of cats. It's easy to understand why Mickey and Minnie would consider this one a horror movie!

6. **Toy Story Midway Mania!:** The barcode on the Toy Story Midway Games Play Set is numbered 121506, referring to the date Toy Story Midway Mania was officially announced as Hollywood Studios' newest attraction.

7. **Streets of America:** The red fire hydrant next to the Chevrolet Building opens at random, with a cooling shower of water that children and children-at-heart can't resist.

8. **Muppet*Vision 3D:** The poster hanging from the ceiling in the pre-show area is a fitting memorial to the Muppets creator, Jim Henson, Muppetized, and with a movie camera lens around his neck.

9. **Stage 1 Company Store:** The clothesline above the cash register and the upper-floor hotel rooms are references to *The Great Muppet Caper* movie, with the addition of a pair of Mickey Mouse's shorts.

10. **Star Tours: The Adventures Continue:** The letters above the top circle on the panel to the right of the Information board read, 2R-OP3C. Read them backward and you have the names of *Star Wars'* two most famous droids.

11. *Indiana Jones Epic Stunt Spectacular:* The symbol on the tail of the German Flying Wing airplane isn't a swastika, though your eye is fooled into thinking it is. Instead, it's a combination of the background of the Nazi flag and the Luftwaffe insignia, the Balkan Cross.

12. *Fantasmic!:* The riverboat ferrying the characters at the end of the show is a replica of the boat in *Steamboat Willie*. Notice who is up in the wheelhouse piloting the boat?

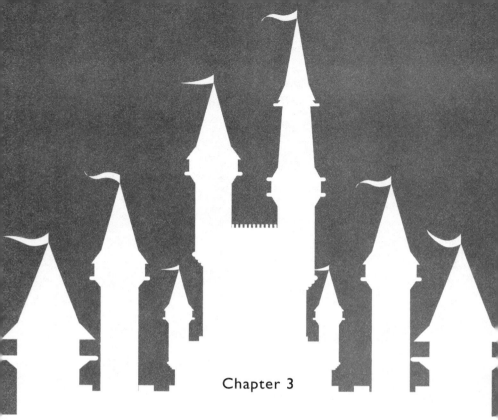

Chapter 3

Disney's Hollywood Studios

"Welcome to the Hollywood that never was and always will be," or so said Michael Eisner, chairman of Walt Disney Company when Disney–MGM Studios opened in 1989. Enter the studios and you are placed firmly amid the glamour of Hollywood during its golden age, surrounded by sights, sounds, and characters that would have been familiar to the likes of Clark Gable, Rita Hayworth, Marilyn Monroe, and Richard Burton—the brightest stars of the '30s, '40s, and '50s.

Walk down any street in the park and you're likely to run across a starlet hoping to be discovered, a soon-to-be-famous director looking for extras for his blockbuster film, and public workers who just know their big break is right around the corner. On one side is a rendition of the theater where now-famous movies debuted, and farther on you pass the restaurant where everyone who was anyone dined, hoping to see and be seen. While the original concept for the studios has been diluted over the years, the allure of being in that most glittering of towns and the pull you feel on your heartstrings when high drama is played out on stage and screen is not the stuff of make-believe; it's alive, vibrant, and immensely convincing. To be a star or to see the stars; the choice is yours!

And now, the scene is set, you know your inspiration, and you have excellent direction. Ready? *Action!*

Hollywood Boulevard

One of the first elements greeting guests as they enter Disney's Hollywood Studios is the Crossroads of the World information kiosk, its spire rising high above Hollywood Boulevard. The crossroads is a replica of the original Crossroads of the World in Hollywood, California, with the addition of a **1930s version of Mickey Mouse** standing proudly on top. Not only does the kiosk serve the functional purpose of providing park maps and various necessities to guests, but it also serves a less obvious purpose. Mickey has one ear higher than the other and his right hand is outstretched. What is he doing up there? His copper ear is grounded and acts as a lightning rod.

As you make your way down Hollywood Boulevard, you'll notice Magic Kingdom isn't the only park with a reason to peek in the windows. Remember to glance at the **upper-story windows** along Hollywood Boulevard and Sunset Boulevard to see who is advertising their services.

When you reach the junction of Hollywood Boulevard and Sunset Boulevard, stand in front of the Tip Board and look down at the half-oval plate in the pavement. It is marked **Est. 1928**, the year Mickey Mouse was first featured in the cartoon short *Steamboat Willie*.

Now turn around and look behind you at the building across the road from the Tip Board. It has the 1928 reference, too, at the top of its rather bland façade. Most of the shops and façades in Hollywood Studios are based on real buildings, and this one takes its inspiration from the **Culver City Ivy Substation** in Culver City, California, a former train station that found its second life as a live-performance theater.

You will see **1928** on various buildings all over Hollywood Studios, so keep an eye out for them. To get you started, Hollywood & Vine restaurant across from Echo Lake is another location marked with Mickey's debut date. See how many more you can find as you tour the park.

Keystone Clothiers, on the left-hand side of Hollywood Boulevard, honors silent film director, producer, and actor, Mack Sennett, who opened Keystone Studios in Los Angeles in 1912. Two of Keystone Pictures most famous properties were Charlie Chaplin and the Keystone Kops. His former studio is now a historic Los Angeles monument.

Sunset Boulevard

As you walk along Sunset Boulevard you can't help but notice suitcases have been left along the curb near Villains in

Vogue. Take a look at the names on the luggage tags. Gilbert London and Carolyn Crosson are characters from the made-for-television movie *Tower of Terror*, starring Steve Guttenberg and Kirsten Dunst.

If you think Carthay Circle Theatre gift shop, on the corner of Sunset Boulevard and Highland, just before the Theater of the Stars, *must* be a replica of something important, you would be right. It was inspired by the real **Carthay Circle Theatre**, where *Snow White and the Seven Dwarfs*, Walt Disney's first full-length animated film, debuted. Had it not been for the success of that movie, Walt Disney's financial future would have been seriously in doubt, as he invested nearly everything he had in production costs.

As you make your way toward the end of the street, pause to look at the red trolley parked in front of Sunset Market Ranch. The trolley has a clever hidden date on the front and the side. Sunset Boulevard opened on June 2, 1994, and the date is commemorated as the trolley's number, **694**. Just a few weeks later, on July 22, 1994, the screams coming from the Tower of Terror would begin.

Imagine That!

It took ingenuity and determination to bring the *Beauty and the Beast* show to the parks. First, Imagineer Ron Logan had to sell the idea of a Broadway show to then-CEO Michael Eisner. Logan remembers the pitch: "I saw parts of the movie, which wasn't out yet, and I saw rough sketches, and wrote a memo to Michael Eisner saying we should take the show to Broadway. He felt it wasn't quite our thing, but he called me and said, 'What about this *Beauty and the Beast* idea? What do we do about the characters? What about the music? What do we do that's magical?' He was vacationing in Aspen and asked me to come and make a presentation. I was scheduled to arrive during the last two hours of the last day of his trip, so I thought, 'I'm doomed.' Jim Steinmeyer, a brilliant illusion master with Walt Disney Imagineering, worked with me to create some special illusions, including a floating rose, and we decided to make Chip, with a child from Aspen inside, using a trick so that his feet wouldn't show. Curtains were set up in the room, the lights were dimmed, and when the curtain opened Chip said, 'Hi Michael! I'm Chip, and I want to go to Broadway!' Afterward, Michael Eisner said 'How did you do that?' I just smiled and said, 'It's magic.' I knew I had him."

Tower of Terror

When you reach the end of Sunset Boulevard, you can't help but notice Hollywood Studios' most easily recognized attraction. Tower of Terror is a massive edifice filled with secrets, some fascinating, some just downright creepy. The Imagineers meant for the attraction to be a horror story, but also a mystery; something scary, but also beautiful.

The plaque on the stone gate on the left side of the walkway leading to the Tower of Terror reads, **Sunset Hills Estate, Est. 1928**, another reference to Mickey Mouse's debut. The gate is a replica of the East Gate entry to Hollywoodland residential estates in Los Angeles, which stood at the base of the hill on which the famous Hollywoodland sign (later just Hollywood after the last four letters were knocked down) was located. The gate had a similar plaque reading, Hollywoodland, Est.1923, which was the year the Hollywoodland sign went up.

One hidden gem can be found straight away. Immediately after you enter the lobby, look at the wall directly to the right of the concierge desk. The Hollywood Tower Hotel has been awarded the AAA (American Automobile Association) **13-Diamond award**, but AAA's real rating system only goes up to five diamonds. It's just a little nudge toward the superstitious and the beginnings of an inescapable sense of foreboding.

There is evidence all around you that the tower was quickly abandoned. Not only have all the clocks stopped at **8:50 P.M.**, the fateful moment lightning struck the building, but guests playing **mahjong** have abandoned their game, **luggage** has been left in the lobby, **unread mail** remains in the designated room slots behind the reception desk, and a French visitor has left her **translation book** on a table near the sofa.

If you have a sharp eye, you may see a **lipstick stain** on the champagne glass sitting on the table next to the wall, with a bottle of champagne next to it. If you can't see it with the naked eye, snap a quick picture with the zoom feature on your camera or phone.

The **folded newspaper** on the reception counter appears to have been left by the gentleman who also left his hat, his coat, and his room key. Notice the date on the paper: It's October 31, 1939.

When you are directed to the preshow room, take note of the **telephone** on a small table immediately to the left. Whoever was on the phone certainly left in a hurry, not even bothering to hang up.

Imagine That!

Eric Jacobson, producer–art director for *The Twilight Zone* Tower of Terror, talks about the decisions faced by WDI when creating an attraction based on a popular cultural icon: "We really had a challenge trying to figure out what the Fifth Dimension scene should be. That's the part of the ride where the elevator car goes horizontally through space. No one had ever realized what the Fifth Dimension was in *The Twilight Zone*; they had just talked about it. We took a lot of the elements of the opening of the show and some of the specific story points that we had created for our ride and mixed them up. We found another art director to help us realize what the mission should be, then we probably did four or five full-scale mockups of that scene. Each time we said, 'No that's not right,' until we got to the final one and said, 'Okay, now we've got it. That's what we're going to do.'"

If you are directed to the preshow room on the left side of the lobby, notice the **Air Mail envelope** on the table, addressed to Frank J. Resch, MD, postmarked 1939 from Gettysburg, Pennsylvania. Frank J. Resch, born in Philadelphia, was a real-life doctor who lived at 5750 Spaulding Avenue in Chicago until his death in 1946. Alas, the Disney connection has been lost, as Walt Disney Imagineering can no longer recall the reason for the letter's inclusion. Still, it's a fascinating link to a man who once had reason for "visiting" the Hollywood Tower Hotel.

Once inside the library, where Rod Serling tells you the story of the tower (some of it in his own voice, which was painstakingly pieced together, in part from *The Twilight Zone* episode "It's a Good Life"), you may recognize props representing various show episodes. Above the bookcase next to the TV in the library you'll see the **demonic popup device** from "The Nick of Time" episode; the **metal robot** from "The Invaders" sits on the ledge above you; a pair of glasses with shattered lenses rest on a stack of books, recalling the episode "Time Enough at Last"; an **envelope** with the name Mary on the front from the episode "A World of His Own"; and the book from the "To Serve Man" episode (during which the townspeople were horrified to discover the alien's benevolent-looking book was actually a cookbook!) is lying face-up on a shelf at the back of the room on the right-hand side. Things do move, so look around if they mysteriously disappear.

There are other *Twilight Zone* references here, too. The **trumpet** sitting on top of a page of sheet music in the library recalls the episode titled "A Passage for Trumpet," in which Joey Crown, convinced he will never amount to anything, throws himself in front of a truck after selling his beloved trumpet to a pawn shop. He ends up in limbo and has to make a decision between life and death.

As you make the final turn toward the elevators in the basement's right-hand queue, notice the word **Danger** written on the pipeline overhead. You can't say you haven't been warned!

Just after you enter the ride elevator, look for the **safety inspection certificate** signed by Mr. Cadwallader, indicating the elevator is in good working order. The certificate is dated October 31, 1939, the day the Tower Hotel opened (and, of course, a spooky reference to Halloween night). The certificate commemorates an episode of *Twilight Zone* titled "Escape Clause," in which Cadwallader, the devil in disguise, grants immortality to Walter Bedeker in exchange for his soul should he later choose not to live. The inspection certificate is number 10259, the numeric version of October 2, 1959, and refers to the date the first *Twilight Zone* episode aired. Now that you know the elevator has passed inspection, take your seat and venture into the terrifying unknown!

Besides highlighting the 1939 version of elegant dining (grapefruit with a maraschino cherry, anyone?), the menu on the wall to the right of the Sunset Room, just past the counter where guests can purchase pictures, holds a few hidden gems. Note the items **Whitefish Matheson**, **Rack of Lamb Johnson**, and **Polonaise Beaumont**. These refer to *Twilight Zone* screenwriters Richard Matheson (sixteen episodes), George

Clayton Johnson (five episodes), and Charles Beaumont (twenty-two episodes). **Gateau Chocolate au Rodman** honors Rodman "Rod" Serling, creator, screenwriter, executive producer, and host of *The Twilight Zone*.

Rock 'n' Roller Coaster

Just around the bend lies another chance to scream for all you're worth. Rock 'n' Roller Coaster represents a bit of a departure from Disney's usual family-friendly style, and it brought more teen-appeal to the park when the ride opened in 1999.

Fascinating Fact

What you are in for when you board your stretch limo? Get ready for a zero-to-sixty launch in only 2.8 seconds, nearly five Gs of force (the space shuttle only reached three Gs at liftoff!), a corkscrew, two rollover loops, and Aerosmith blaring in your ear courtesy of five speakers . . . per passenger!

The Rock Rack magazine dispenser next to the Parking Available sign contains the Central Florida tourism magazine *Enjoy Florida*. Which edition? The Walt Disney World edition, of course!

The delivery address for G-Force Records, just to the left of the light fixture on the building across the alley reads **1401 Flower Street**. Why did Imagineers choose that street and number? It's the address of Walt Disney Imagineering in Glendale, California.

You would think the name **Sam Andreas & Son** on the Construction Crew Only sign hanging on the fence just before the bend in the queue that leads to the loading area must be an Imagineer signature, right? But that would be "faulty" thinking. It's just a playful version of earthquake-prone San Andreas, California.

Buena Vista Fence Co has a sign on the chain link fence, just before the turn toward the loading area. By now you know the phone number must mean something, and you're right. If you add the correct area code the phone number goes straight to the switchboard for Walt Disney Imagineering.

You're almost to the loading area and although you may not know what to expect from the ride, there is no doubt about what is expected of you. Take a look at the blue guitar-shaped sign giving safety instructions for guests while riding. There is a humorous notation at the bottom, **"Thank you vera much,"** a subtle nod to Elvis Presley and his slight variation on the use of the English language.

Imagine That!

Walt Disney's spirit is very much alive in how WDI operates, even today. Imagineer Eddie Sotto, with WDI from 1986 to 1999, explains, "You're there to take everything further and push the envelope. That was Walt. The public expects you to take what could only be in a movie and make it real. Quite a challenge. So you have to have an attitude that allows you to be flexible as to all kinds of ways of achieving the fantasy for the guest. So it takes Walt's risk-taking process to get there, and some courage. I was told once, 'never underestimate someone who overestimates themselves.' When I stopped laughing it hit me: If you're not aware that you're incapable of something, then it's more likely you'll make it happen!"

Courtyard

Each of the parks has a reference to its opening day, and you may be wondering where Disney–MGM Studios' (using the park's original name) opening day is commemorated. Walk back to the central courtyard and look for the large bronze statue of a producer with a movie camera. The park's dedication plaque has returned after disappearing for a few years, and is now located near the bronze statue of the photographer on Hollywood Boulevard. Michael Eisner dedicated the park on May 1, 1989.

Fascinating Fact

Tinker Bell, one of Disney's most beloved characters, nearly became a footnote in animation history. Margaret Kerry remembers, "After *Peter Pan*, Tinker Bell was not going to do anything else. Then Walt Disney decided to make this theme park in a place called Anaheim. The consensus of opinion was, 'God help us! Anaheim? Walt's going to lose his shirt.' Roy Disney was asked to tell Walt not to use any of the licensed characters that were generating most of the company's money, because if any of these characters were involved with a project that failed, they were going to be worthless. Walt thought about it and said, 'I'm going to use Jiminy Cricket and Tinker Bell in the park. Will that satisfy them?' and that's the reason those two characters came back to life."

Farther along, acting as the park's original central icon, the Chinese Theater probably looks familiar to many guests. It is a replica of the Hollywood landmark, **Grauman's Chinese Theatre**, which opened in 1927. Sid Grauman, original owner of Grauman's Chinese Theatre in California, came up with the idea of casting stars' footprints in cement, starting with Mary Pickford, Norma Talmadge, and Douglas Fairbanks. He also created the idea of the ultra-glamorous Hollywood movie premiere.

The two stone **Foo Dogs** guarding the theater's front door were carved by Chinese artists and are exact replicas of those at Grauman's Chinese Theatre.

The Great Movie Ride

The Great Movie Ride is your chance to ride the movies, and a grand spectacle waits on the other side of the marquee. But first, take the time to inspect each of the props as you walk through the lobby. There are many cinematic treasures here, including **the dress Scarlett O'Hara wore** in the opening scene of *Gone with the Wind*. Other props in the queue are original, too, but all are displayed on a rotating basis, so they may be different each time you visit.

The Great Movie Ride offers two distinct scenarios, one with a **cowboy theme**, and the other with a **gangster theme**, so if you have a preference, ask a Cast Member to direct you to the correct ride vehicle.

As soon as you enter the James Cagney scene just after the *Mary Poppins* setting, look at the posters on the wall to your left. The bottom of one of them has been torn, and you can see **Mickey Mouse's shoes** peeking out from behind.

Keep looking to your left as you pass through the gangster scene. You may catch a glimpse of **Mickey's silhouette** in the right-hand corner of the Western Chemical Company building's upper window. If you don't see it when you first enter the scene, look back as your ride vehicle begins to move again after the gunfight.

Watch for **movement behind the curtain** on the second floor of the hotel as you enter Gangster Alley. One of the hotel guests is in big trouble, and he's being threatened by a man with a tommy gun!

As you're watching the hotel scene unfold, listen to actor James Cagney as Tom Powers on the right side of the alley. You may hear him mention he is looking for **Puddy Nose**. His comment is a reference to the 1931 movie *The Public Enemy* in which Puddy Nose is Tom's mentor for a short time.

During the gunfight in Gangster Alley, one of the **bullets ricochets off of a sign** on your right, making it swing back and forth.

Those **Gold Shield Whisky** crates on the left side of Gangster Alley are a tribute to the 1939 crime thriller *The Roaring Twenties*, starring James Cagney and Humphrey Bogart as soldiers-turned-bootleggers.

Patrick J. Ryan's Bar is another reference to *The Public Enemy* in which James Cagney gets into the bootlegging business after a meeting in Paddy Ryan's bar.

Also in the gangster version, notice the **license plate number** on the car in the shootout scene. It's 021-429, a variation on February 14, 1929, the date of the infamous Saint Valentine's Day Massacre in Chicago.

Imagine That!

The further you delve into the small details that bring the larger aspects of an attraction to life, the more you appreciate the passion Disney Imagineers pour into their work. But what happens when a design element outlives its usefulness? Mark Hervat, manager, Art and Design, Creative Entertainment, says, "It's always good to be passionate about your work, but it only goes so far. Like at movie premieres; you work hard on the sculptures and backdrops that will go up outside the theater and then, while people are in the premiere, there are guys outside with chainsaws cutting them up. You think, 'Oh no! I worked forever on that!'"

If you opt for the interactive cowboy version of the ride, **watch for smoke** when the bank blows up. It comes right through the barn walls.

You may wonder if Wyatt Earp will come strolling out of the scenery, and your expectation wouldn't be unreasonable.

The town you travel through certainly recalls Tombstone, Arizona, "the town too tough to die." **Cochise County Court House** (the county where Tombstone is actually located) is on your right, covered in Wells Fargo posters offering rewards for the Most Wanted outlaws. The *Tombstone Epitaph* is on your left, a re-creation of the real-life *Tombstone Epitaph*, which carried the story of the gunfight at the OK Corral in the October 27, 1881, edition. Curiously enough, the University of Arizona's Department of Journalism still publishes a paper under that name, with the tag line "No Tombstone Is Complete Without Its Epitaph."

If you look to the right in the same scene, on the Cochise County Court House building, just past Clint Eastwood, you'll see a sign advertising **Ransom Stoddard**, Attorney. Senator Ransom Stoddard was a character played by Jimmy Stewart in the 1962 John Wayne movie *The Man Who Shot Liberty Valance.*

Guests with an exceptionally quick eye may notice some of the hieroglyphics on the walls in the Egyptian scene have rather surprising icons. See if you can locate **R2-D2 and C-3PO** from the Star Wars movie series (look directly across from Indiana Jones, on the left-hand side of the tram, just about at eye level near the snakes). You will have to look quickly, so you may want to seek this one out on a second ride-through.

A large hieroglyph featuring Donald Duck as an Egyptian servant offering a slice of cheese to **Pharaoh Mickey Mouse** can be found on the left-hand wall in the Well of Souls scene, directly in the corner of the third tier of hieroglyphs, just before you leave the area. Again, look quickly!

You're going to have to look quickly to see this, and also sit at the end of the row on the left side of the ride vehicle. The first monitor you pass on your left includes lines of statistics, but ignore them and look at the bottom two paragraphs of inline text. The first of these two paragraphs reads, **"The Nostromo welcomes all aliens visiting today from the Glendale Galaxy. We hope you have a pleasant stay with us**.**"** Glendale Galaxy refers to Glendale, California, headquarters for Walt Disney Imagineering. The bottom line of text in the final paragraph reads, **"Time till next special effects failure . . . 45.8 years."**

Fascinating Fact

Hieroglyphics are tricky. Until the Rosetta Stone was discovered, with two known languages to compare to the unknown hieroglyphic text, archaeologists found it nearly impossible to decipher the symbols, in part due to the fact that ancient Egyptians were more concerned with aesthetics than they were with continuity. They believed a word should look pleasing, which meant the symbols may not be in a strict order, they may face a different direction (though left-facing is most common), several characters could be used to represent the same letter, and they were subject to the writer's artistic interpretation. To top it all off, vowels were generally left out. An interesting idiosyncrasy of the hieroglyphics in the Great Movie Ride is that symbols that would traditionally face left, since hieroglyphics are read right-to-left, are instead facing right. Although it is not the case in the attraction, this retrograde text was often used when one of the characters in the sentence was important, such as a symbol representing a pharaoh. Out of "respect," all the symbols would face him.

If you are sitting on the extreme left side of the tram, you may also see the screen titled **Crew Status Roster**, which shows a listing of the Imagineers and designers of the Great

Movie Ride. Notice each crew member's current status; some are listed as missing while others have humorous notations next to their names.

Next, look to your right. There is a **wind chime** similar to the one in the movie *Aliens* hanging in front of the second space suit.

You may recall having seen the rear half of a **Lockheed Electra 12A airplane** as you made your way around the Jungle Cruise at Magic Kingdom, and you certainly can't miss the front half, which features prominently in the *Casablanca* scene. It isn't the original plane used in the movie, however. The Lockheed Electra 12A in the movie was actually a mockup, not a real airplane.

You will be able to see Munchkin Land shortly before you enter the first *Wizard of Oz* scene. Notice how the Yellow Brick Road forms itself into the letter **O** at the beginning, and then trails off toward the second scene. When you reach the scene with Dorothy and her friends, look at the Yellow Brick Road where it ends in front of the Emerald City. Notice how it forms the letter **Z**, effectively tying both scenes to the word *Oz*.

Pay particular attention to the **Wicked Witch** when she makes her dramatic appearance shortly after your tram stops. Prior to the A-100 technology used in making the witch, Audio-Animatronics could not move quickly without looking unnatural, giving her the distinction of being the first to exhibit more natural movements. As amazing as this technology is, it still takes an entire week to program fifteen seconds of motion.

Imagine That!

Many attractions are so beautifully presented that it is difficult to single out the smaller details. But they are no less important, as Eric

Jacobson, Senior Vice President of Creative Development at WDI, attests: "I was producer–art director on the Great Movie Ride, and our team researched all those movies that we included in the ride, over and over again. We read books and watched them on video. Back in the 1980s the equipment that we had to work with wasn't as sophisticated as it is now, but we printed out black-and-white frames from a lot of the movies so that we could really slow it down and look to see, for example, exactly what the Wicked Witch of the West's costumes looked like. We noticed as we looked at the film in slow frame-by-frame that she actually has a purse around her waist that, probably, nobody has really noticed. So we said, that's a neat detail we want to include to make sure her costume is as authentic as it could possibly be, even though it would be very simple to elimi-nate something like that because most people probably won't even notice it in the attraction."

Animation Courtyard

Animation Courtyard originally debuted as the working heart of Disney's Hollywood Studios, a place where guests could watch Disney artists as they went about their craft, take a tram ride past a division of the wardrobe and con-struction departments, and get a sense of the true behind-the-scenes operations that bring the movies to life.

The **black-and-white photograph** you see to the left of the stage in the Magic of Disney Animation is Walt Disney as a teenager. Neat little inclusion, isn't it?

When the show lets out, take note of the animator's setting as you walk toward the interactive area of the building. The **paint jars** on the wall represent all the colors used in the animated movie *Sleeping Beauty*.

Minnie Mouse Meet and Greet

As of 2013, Minnie Mouse has a meet-and-greet location, and it's chock-full of subtle references. The waiting area before you meet Miss Mouse is lined with movie posters, and if you love Disney history references, you'll want to have a look.

The credits at the bottom of the **Ailurophobia poster** mention several Disney characters, as well as a twist on the term "Disney-Vision." In the mode of the movie *Arachnophobia*, which refers to the fear of spiders, *Ailurophobia* is a reference to the fear of cats. It's easy to understand why Mickey and Minnie would consider this one a horror movie. The poster even mentions the movie is based on the novel *Peur des Chats*, which means "fear of cats" in French. Also notice *Mickey's PhilharMagic* provided the film's music.

The Jungle Cruise poster mentions several Disney greats, including Disney Legend Harper Goff as the movie's Producer; horticulturist Bill Evans as Director; Marc Davis, in charge of Set Design; and Chief Creative Officer John Lasseter and Vice President of Creative Design Patrick Brennan as Skippers.

Theater of the Stars, mentioned at the top of the poster, refers to the park's theater on Sunset Boulevard, and the date **July 17** was Disneyland's opening day. **Trader Sam** is also mentioned on the poster. He is the original "head salesman" guests saw at the end of the Jungle Cruise journey in Disneyland, selling shrunken heads.

Further Disney greats receive a mention on the **Mouse Pacific** poster. **The Sherman Brothers** obviously refers to the legendary musical duo Robert and Richard Sherman, who wrote such memorable tunes as "it's a small world (after all)," "There's a Great Big Beautiful Tomorrow," and songs for the movie *Mary Poppins*, achieving 125 songs in all.

Fulton Burley, Wally Boag, Thurl Ravenscroft, and Ernie Newton are also honored, with their first names substituted for those of the birds Michael, José, Fritz, and Pierre from the Enchanted Tiki Room. Why? Because each of them voiced the bird they are named for on the poster.

The Bride of Frankenollie mentions several Disney characters, but the real gem here is in the title. "Frankenollie" refers to Disney animators Frank Thomas and Ollie Johnston, both among Walt Disney's celebrated team of Nine Old Men.

Imagine That!

Gene Columbus recalls the first time he met Walt Disney, and the impact that meeting had on him: "Having started my career as a performer, I went to Hollywood so I could be in the movies but learned very quickly that it was not as easy as it looks. In order to even go to an audition you had to be in the union, but you could not join the union unless you were cast in a film. After a few years of frustration I snuck into an audition of *Babes in Toyland* at Walt Disney Productions and was selected, but once they found out I was not in the union I was dropped from the call. However, the Disney casting director saw this and stepped in, offering me the opportunity to be a stand-in just to get me in the union. I was thrilled, but had little idea of what I was supposed to do, so I waited until I was told what to do and how to do it. Fact was, I only had to stand there for the lights and camera to be focused. When the crew broke for coffee I felt very unimportant, so I would wait until everyone got their coffee and then I would get a cup and wander around trying to see if anyone wanted to talk. On the fourth day I came in early, but waited until most of the crew had their coffee as I considered myself to be not very important. As I was putting the cream in my coffee I looked back at the person who got in line behind me and he extended his hand and said, 'Hello, I'm Walt Disney.' Everything after that is a blur as he asked questions about where I was from and what I was doing.

I have no idea what I said except that I kept calling him Mr. Disney! I often tell people that Walt Disney did not presume that I knew who he was, and he wanted to know about me, the most unimportant person on that sound stage. The man whose name was on the gate I entered through that morning made me feel important."

Who can forget Gene Kelly singing in the rain in the 1952 movie of the same name? If you ever had the wistful desire to dance in a downpour, you will have your chance when you reach the intersection directly across from *Lights, Motors, Action!* just to the right of the San Francisco backdrop. The street lamp on the corner has an **umbrella** attached. Stand on the black pad and pull the umbrella's handle for a delightful surprise and a terrific picture for the family photo album.

Imagine That!

Although his first meeting with Walt Disney was awkward, Ron Logan recalls, "I met Walt for the second time in Squaw Valley during the 1960 Winter Olympics. I was in a fanfare trumpet group and we played each time a medal was given away. Walt had a chalet, which he opened to performers, and we could get a burger or a Coke there. Walt always treated everyone great. It was not about the money; it was about being treated well."

Pixar Studios

Pixar Studios has a permanent place in Walt Disney World, solidifying the Disney-Pixar merger in high style with Toy Story Midway Mania! The attention to detail is outstanding, and you'll find lots of hidden gems here in the land "where toys come to work and play."

You will recall many of the buildings in Disney's Hollywood Studios are based on real structures, and in the case of Pixar Studios, that couldn't be more true. The large gateway you pass through is a replica of Pixar's gateway in Emeryville, California, and the **bricks** used throughout the area were chosen to exactly match those at the Emeryville animation studio.

Toy Story Midway Mania!

As soon as you pass by the pale blue **Crayola crayon** just before you enter the attraction, you get a sense of having shrunk to the size of a toy. Once you reach the boarding area, you have symbolically entered Andy's room and you're interacting with his toys, who have discovered a new Midway game under the bed.

Shortly after you enter the attraction you will come across the first of Andy's assortment of books, with more scattered throughout the queue and the boarding area. Most of them are books that were **influential childhood reading**, such as *The Boy Scout Handbook*, *Babes in Toyland*, and the Little Reader Storybook series, or **Pixar short films**, such as *Red's Dream* and *Knick Knack*. You will also see many of the same books if you pay close attention to Andy's bookshelf in the *Toy Story* movie. However, there are a few exceptions. On your right-hand side shortly after you enter the queue are *Frogs: Where Did They All Go?* by Tom Carlisle and *Magic Made Easy* by J. Ranft. Tom Carlisle is Pixar's Animation Studios facilities director and J. Ranft memorializes Joe Ranft, Disney and Pixar storyboard supervisor before his death in 2005. Ranft was nominated for an Academy Award for Best Writing, Screenplay Written Directly for the Screen, for his work on the *Toy Story* movie. Just across from the boarding area a stack of books painted on the wall includes the book *Smyrl Smyrl Twist and Twirl*, which refers to Eliot Smyrl, a member of Pixar's modeling and animation systems development team that worked on the first *Toy Story* movie.

As you make your slow, winding way toward the loading area you will pass by many of Andy's Lincoln Log creations. Some of them give the distinct impression that Andy may have been a budding Imagineer. Like most children, he doesn't necessarily have the engineering part of the equation exactly right, but he did come up with a creative solution. Those blobs of blue and pink you see at the corners of some of the structures are meant to be **Play-Doh** and **Silly Putty**, used as a quick fix to keep Andy's constructions upright.

You will also notice Andy is a prolific artist, as evidenced by all his drawings throughout the queue and the crayons scattered around. Look at the **points of the crayons** as you walk past. Some have been used extensively, while others haven't been used at all.

A delightful bit of Imagineering whimsy comes in the form of a balsawood airplane, along the right-hand side of the queue. While most people are familiar with the inexpensive childhood toy, this one has a rather special name. It's a **Blue Sky** flyer, in reference to Imagineering's Blue Sky Studios and the process of brainstorming—called the blue-sky phase—used by Imagineers when creating new concepts for shows and attractions.

Imagine That!

When designing new attractions, the Imagineers take their inspiration from many places. Chrissie Allen, senior show producer, recalls the initial process for Toy Story Midway Mania! "We were really inspired by the Buzz Lightyear ride. How can we make it more competitive and more repeatable? You may notice every time you stop at a game, the vehicle records your score along with your percentage. That's the kind of technology we love nowadays. It's an invisible technology; guests have no idea how we're doing it, and that's what we like to achieve. It is a combination of these things and the combination of a lot of exciting technologies wrapped in a new way. A lot of this is still old technology. It's a bar ride (meaning, the ride vehicles are linked together by a bar) that has spin turrets, and they have been around for many years. But we've added computer technology, gaming technology, and the latest projection techniques, and that's what takes us to a new level."

Acting as a carnival game barker, **Mr. Potato Head** certainly grabs your attention as you walk through the queue, but that's not the only thing he can grab. The technology used to create him is so advanced, he holds the distinction of being the first Audio-Animatronic character that can remove and replace one of its own body parts. He's also the first to have a mouth that looks like it forms real words as he is speaking and eyes that look directly at individual guests.

Some of Andy's handiwork can be found on the wall just after you turn the corner past Mr. Potato Head, but before you pick up your 3D glasses. Andy has painted some of his favorite characters, including a finger-painting of Nemo from *Finding Nemo*.

Just before you enter the game itself, you will see the Toy Story Midway Games Play Set on the right-hand wall, with a bar code on the bottom left side. There are several numbers around the bar code, as you would expect, but the number on the bottom left of the bar code is the **number 121506**. That number refers to the date Toy Story Midway Mania! was officially announced as Hollywood Studios' newest attraction in the making.

Your focus will be firmly on the game after you board your ride vehicle and set off for some midway mania, but once you have launched your final dart at Woody's Rootin' Tootin' Shootin' Gallery and Buzz Lightyear tallies up your score, notice the split-fingered **hand gesture** he makes as he says goodbye. It's the Vulcan "live long and prosper" sign, which you also saw in Leonard Nimoy's cement handprints at the Great Movie Ride.

Buzz Lightyear is multilingual, as evidenced by him **speaking Spanish** when you reach the prize booth at the end of the ride. It's a reference to the movie *Toy Story 3*, when Buzz had some serious language issues.

Imagine That!

Appealing to young and old alike was a primary goal for the Imagineers during the design process for Toy Story Midway Mania! Senior Show Producer for the attraction, Sue Bryan, says, "When you look at how broad our audience is, we really wanted to make this attraction appeal to everybody and also make everyone feel like they were successful and had a good time. It's no fun to play a game and feel like, 'Oh, I don't play games and I'm not going to do well.' We started play-testing and we had very simple software mockups to try to find out what's fun for everybody and how could we make different levels of challenge so that a three-year-old who can't aim, a teenager who plays games all the time, and my father who has never played a game in his life can literally get into the carnival tram, pull the string, and be successful from the start. So if you look at the scenes, the different sizes of targets, the different movements of the target you can see we spent an unbelievable amount of time tuning that and testing with people. It's really a passion for us to make sure that everybody got off smiling and feeling like they did a good job."

Although you will be happily chattering away about your score and how quickly you can get through the queue again for a second ride, there is one final touch that will pull gently at the heartstrings of anyone over the age of forty. Just before you leave the unloading area, you will pass by an enormous Little Golden Book, open so that you can see the front and back covers. Like many of the toys and games found throughout the queue and in Andy's room, Little Golden Books played a significant literary role in many Americans' early childhood. Since the first title, *The Poky Little Puppy*, debuted in 1942, more than 2 billion Little Golden Books have been sold, and it's a safe bet to say, they all eventually had **tattered corners** from being so well loved, just as the one here in Andy's room does.

Streets of America

The hustle and bustle found in any big city in America has been beautifully captured along Streets of America, both in terms of the architecture and the ambient sounds. As you walk along the street, you can hear streetcars, police whistles, noisy buses, and the hurried sounds of daily life. A wonderful touch, don't you think?

During the worst heat of summer, big cities such as New York and Chicago provide welcome relief from blistering temperatures by opening up the fire hydrants in many neighborhoods, creating a perfect water fountain for overheated residents to run through. The red **fire hydrant** in the alley two blocks up from the San Francisco backdrop, next to the Chevrolet Building, opens at random, with a cooling (or possibly jolting) shower of water that children and children-at-heart can't resist.

The people of Hollywood Studios certainly like to write on the sidewalk. Along with the handprints and footprints at the Chinese Theater and the Hollywood Hills Amphitheater, the citizens (park designers) living along Streets of America across from Chinatown carved their names in the sidewalk's wet cement for all of posterity.

As you pass by Sal's Pawn Shop near the *Honey, I Shrunk the Kids* playground, peek in the window and you'll see several watches hanging from a stand. Among them is an early **1960s Mickey Mouse watch**. Notice Mickey's gloves are red, and one of his hands is missing, so whoever buys it should get a good deal.

Whether you are into character meet-and-greets or not, take a walk through the short queue to meet monsters Mike and Sulley. There is a sign on the right-hand wall that reads, **Top 10 Ways to Get Fired**. Each reason is humorous, but number 9 refers to Glenn Kim, a production artist on the 2001 movie *Monsters, Inc.* It makes you wonder what he got up to, doesn't it?

Honey, I Shrunk the Kids Movie Set Adventure

If you have children in your group, you're likely to spend some time exploring the *Honey, I Shrunk the Kids* Movie Set Adventure, a larger-than-life playground filled with all things climbing, jumping, and sliding. Even if you don't have children with you, stop in for some terrific photo opportunities. With the giant dog's face so close to the ground, it's a given you'll want to **stick your hand inside his nose**. Go ahead . . . try it! You may trigger a surprising reaction.

Imagine That!

Ron Logan talks about working under the direction of CEO Michael Eisner: "The number one thing Michael Eisner did for me was, he always said, 'Figure it out.' He didn't tell me how to do things. I also had his phone number in my top pocket and if someone didn't want to do something I took it out, handed it to them, and said, 'Call Eisner and tell him you won't do it.' No one ever did."

Muppet*Vision 3D

As you approach Muppet*Vision (from the Star Tours side), you will see a long wall topped with planters full of flowers. However, one of the planters isn't filled with a bouquet. Instead it's an **ice-cream sundae**. And if you look at the planter at the far end, you'll see that someone already ate the sundae contained in that planter, leaving nothing but the spoon.

Time flies when you're in Walt Disney World but **Gonzo** has taken the idea just a bit too far. Look up at the clock on the front of Muppet*Vision. That's him, hanging from the minute hand.

Just after you enter the Muppet*Vision building, there is a box office to your right. The ticket seller has gone out, but he left a note saying the **key is under the mat**. You know you want to, so go ahead and lift the mat.

Naughty Miss Piggy! She has posed for a **pinup calendar**, which is now on display on the bulletin board to the left of the door in the security guard's room, just after you enter the queue.

Muppet*Vision's preshow holding area is filled with jokes, some of them obvious, some less so. Just after you enter the room, look up at the net filled with red and green squares of Jell-O. It's a pun on the name of Mickey's famous Mouseketeer, Annette Funicello. Get it? **A net full of Jell-O**.

There are several jokes on the clapperboard hanging on the left-hand wall after you enter the Muppet*Vision preshow area. The Scene is **Happiness Hotel**, referring to the hotel in the movie *The Great Muppet Caper*; the Take is **My Wife, Please**! which was comedian Henny Youngman's signature line, variations of which have been used in many Muppet productions; the camera is a **Kodiak Brownie**, a takeoff on the Kodak Brownie camera popular in the early 1900s, but this time with a bear-inspired twist; and the Star is **Ursula Major**, a feminization of Ursa Major, a constellation also known as the Great Bear. It is worth noting the director of this particular film is none other than Fozzie Bear.

Along the wall to the right after you enter the preshow area is the top of a shipping crate, referencing the painting *The Sleepy Zootsy*. Zoot is the saxophone-playing Muppet and the picture in question appeared in Miss Piggy's Art Masterpiece Calendar. *The Sleepy Zootsy* is a takeoff on the famous artist Henri Rousseau's *The Sleeping Gypsy*. You can see the Muppet version of the painting just below the crate top.

Hanging near the ceiling toward the front left-hand side of the preshow area, you'll see a poster of a Muppet that looks oddly familiar. It is a fitting memorial to the Muppets creator, **Jim Henson**, Muppetized, and with a movie camera lens around his neck.

The scene in which Miss Piggy sings "**Dream a Little Dream**" is a nod toward "Mama" Cass Elliot, lead singer for the 1960s group, the Mamas and the Papas. When Cass Elliot branched out on her own she made a promotional commercial upon which the Muppets' scene is based. Cass, however, wore nothing, though the daisies obstructed what shouldn't be shown.

Imagine That!

The Imagineers decided the Muppets would be aware they were being filmed in 3D for the first time. That's why Kermit mentions not using "cheap 3D tricks" and, as the story progresses, their self-consciousness occasionally shows.

Stage 1 Company Store

It may be a gift shop, but it's chock-full of humorous Muppets references. It's easy to tell who each **bus station locker** near the front door belongs to by the personal items they contain. Look for Miss Piggy's girly possessions, Sgt. Floyd Pepper's hippie paraphernalia, and Fozzie Bear's obvious obsession with magic. The setting is a reference to the movie *The Muppets Take Manhattan*.

The **clothesline** above the cash register and the **upper-floor hotel rooms** are references to *The Great Muppet Caper* movie, with the addition of a pair of Mickey Mouse's shorts.

Just above the clothesline, on the second floor, there is a picture of **the Old Curiosity Shop** on Portsmouth Street in Westminster, London. The shop takes its name from the Charles Dickens novel, and the picture is appropriate here as a reference to the Muppets' visit to London in *The Great Muppet Caper*.

As you wander through the shop, take time to read the signs, including **The Five Laws of Show Biz**. There are so many jokes and comical vignettes in here you could spend an hour just looking around.

Star Tours: The Adventures Continue

Star Tours was given an overhaul of galactic proportions, reopening in 2011 as Star Tours: The Adventures Continue with a time frame that is based between the two Star Wars trilogies. While the motion simulator experience remains the same, the story line has changed completely. You're visiting an intergalactic space port from which you'll embark on tours to some of the most popular planets in the Star Wars movies. Former pilot Captain Rex is gone, but with C-3PO and R2-D2 at the helm, what could go wrong?

There is so much happening on the **Information board** located shortly after you enter the queue that you could easily spend an hour taking it all in. The hidden gems you see will depend entirely on when you arrive and how quickly the queue moves.

While you are in the first half of the queue, pay attention to the intercom announcements and to the sales pitches for various intergalactic destinations. The sales pitches are presented by droid **Aly San San**, named for Allison Janney, the actress who voiced the character. Aly San San's look was based on the waitress droid, **WA-7**, from *Star Wars Episode II: Attack of the Clones*.

One of the sales pitches is for a tour to Cloud City, which promises you'll see a special celebration, including **Fantasy in the Sky** fireworks. This refers to the fireworks show that lit up the sky over Magic Kingdom's Cinderella Castle from 1971 until 2003.

As you are queuing toward the boarding area, pay attention to the various pages over the intercom and you may hear a page for **Egroeg Sacul** (George Lucas spelled backward).

Another important announcement may grab your attention while you are queuing, especially if you did not heed the advice to make a note of where you parked when you arrived today. Listen for an announcement asking the owner of a speeder whose license plate has the number **THX**

1138, and would they please remove it from the no-hover zone. *THX 1138* was the first movie made by George Lucas in 1971, an adaptation of a short film he created while at the University of Southern California. THX1138 is also referenced as **Flight 1138 to Coruscant** on the Departures board.

Listen for the announcement addressing **Mot Worrom**. It is a reference to Tom Morrow, using his first and last names spelled backward. You might recall Tom Morrow is a tribute to an Imagineer who worked on the now-extinct Mission to Mars at Magic Kingdom.

While you're facing the Information board, look at the panel to your right. The letters above the top circle read **2R-OP3C**. Read them backward and you have the names of *Star Wars'* two most famous droids.

Just above the lower circle on the same panel, you'll see **N1C7C01**. If you read every other letter, it spells out NCC-1701, the registry number of the starship *Enterprise* of *Star Trek* fame.

Bummer about the **Fralideja settlement** on the planet Mustafar. The weather report on the Information board might dissuade tourists, as the settlement is experiencing some rather intense-looking ash storms.

The next element you come across in the queue is the Starspeeder 1000. You will see the number **1401** in a few locations on the ship, a reference to 1401 Flower Street in Glendale California, which is the street address for Walt Disney Imagineering. The ship you will be boarding is Flight 1401.

The sentence written in Aurebesh just above the name Starspeeder 1000 and just under R2-D2 reads, **Astromech Droid Socket**. The primary purpose of an astromech droid is maintenance and repair, though they are sometimes used as navigators, a role astromech R2-D2 performed in the original *Star Wars* movie.

To the right of R2-D2 is a camera droid, with the designation **IC-360** below him. Say it out loud as "I see 360," indicating the droid can see in every direction. It is also a reference to Disney's filming technique, Circle-Vision 360°.

TK-421 refers to the Imperial Stormtrooper whose battle armor was stolen by Luke Skywalker in the original *Star Wars* movie, prompting the query, "TK-421, why aren't you at your post?" You may also hear his name in a comment made by G2-9T, the luggage scanner droid.

Fascinating Fact

If you would like to learn Aurebesh, there are plenty of websites that feature the alien language's characters. It's surprisingly easy to memorize, so take lots of pictures while you're in the queue at Star Tours and you can translate when you get home.

Just after you enter the second portion of the queue, look immediately to your left. **Captain Rex**, former pilot for Star Tours before the attraction's makeover in 2011, is being shipped back to the factory as defective equipment. He still talks though, so pause for a moment and listen.

Like the Information board, the **luggage scanner** in the second half of the queue is a seemingly endless source of entertainment. **Droid G2-9T** (who says you can call him Roger) is overseeing luggage inspection, with hilarious results. Among the items he finds in unsuspecting travelers' suitcases are golden Mickey ears from Disneyland's 50th Anniversary Celebration; a Goofy hat; Goofy himself; the Mad Hatter's hat; a case full of hands and legs ("because you never see hands solo"); Chip and Dale plush toys; Wall-E; Aladdin's lamp; a Buzz Lightyear toy; Madame Leota's head from the Haunted Mansion attraction; and so much more. He comments on each case, and it's worth letting a few people pass you in the queue if today is busy.

At one point G2-9T says, **"We're not here to change the world,"** a reference to the attraction *Captain EO* at Epcot's Imagination pavilion. He also says, **"And you think about that!"** Ellen uses that sentence in the Universe of Energy attraction's preshow at Epcot.

Watch the screen at the bend in the queue after the luggage scanner. Your fellow travelers can be seen in shadow, and one of them is **R2-D2 wearing a set of Mickey ears**.

Many of the safety spiel elements are takeoffs on the attraction's original safety spiel, including a **child taking a photo of Chewbacca** and the woman reprimanding the child. She recalls the **poofy-haired host** of the previous Star Tours safety video.

Fascinating Fact

Why are guests asked not to put their 3D glasses on when they first enter the Starspeeder? It's not for safety reasons. Instead, when you are asked to look at the Cast Member loading your cabin, a photograph is taken of everyone onboard. And now you know how they capture the image of the Rebel Spy, who might just be you!

As you crash and burn your way through the universe, you may notice some of the comments made throughout your journey are **lines from the Star Wars movies**. You'll be tossed around a lot and may not be able to listen too closely, but if she is on your tour notice Princess Leia's appeal, with a twist on her famous line, "Help me Obi-Wan Kenobi. You're my only hope."

If you pass by Star Tours in the evening when the area is quiet and you listen closely, you may hear **Ewoks** talking, chanting, and drumming. But remember, they only come out after sunset (or around 7:00 during those late sunset months). You can hear them best near the building's entry and at the far end of the forest, an area that normally is unused unless lines are extremely long. Walk back there during slower times when you can stop and listen for a while.

Indiana Jones Epic Stunt Spectacular

High thrills are in store at *Indiana Jones Epic Stunt Spectacular*, where the stunts are real and so is the danger. How does Indy avoid getting speared as he makes his way through the temple to retrieve the golden idol? He actually controls the release of the spears by stepping on **square keypads**, so he knows exactly when they will spring. But yes, they are real and he could get hurt.

There is no doubt about the villains Indiana Jones is dealing with in the movie *Indiana Jones and the Raiders of the Lost Ark*, but the *Indiana Jones Epic Stunt Spectacular* has no direct references to the Nazis. The symbol you see on the tail of the German Flying Wing airplane isn't a swastika, though your eye is fooled into thinking it is, and when the attraction opened it *was* a swastika. It was changed to a combination of the background of the **Nazi flag** and the Luftwaffe insignia, the **Balkan Cross**. Clever, isn't it?

With everything going on above ground, it's easy to miss what's going on beneath your feet. As you pass by the entry to *Indiana Jones Epic Stunt Spectacular*, to the left of the entry, down the path on the right-hand side, there is a well with a sign saying, **Do Not Pull the Rope**. Notice *NOT* has been crossed out. You know what to do!

Echo Lake

When Disney-MGM Studios was being built, the crater that would become Echo Lake was the first thing to go in, and the park grew up around it. Located around a small lake, just as the tiny town of Echo Lake, California, is set around its namesake body of water, this charming area of Hollywood Studios has several opportunities for a snack or a meal, and some lovely hidden magic.

Just across the lagoon, **Gertie the Dinosaur** is more than just a quick snack stop during your Hollywood Studios visit, she is also a tribute to Winsor McCay, a vaudevillian actor who created Gertie as an addition to his show. She was the first animated film featuring a dinosaur in the days before multiplane cameras. It took over 14,400 drawings, done on rice paper, to create the desired effect and give the illusion Gertie was interacting with Mr. McCay.

Fascinating Fact

Gertie the Dinosaur is an example of the architectural style known as California Crazy. Southern California in the 1920s and 1930s flourished with many such roadside curiosities designed to capture the attention of the traveling public as they sped along the highway at a dizzying 35 miles per hour. A giant puppy housing a hot dog stand, bakeries shaped like windmills, massive mushrooms, larger-than-life flowerpots and elephants, even the Great Sphinx of Egypt were a sure-fire way of attracting patrons into an establishment for a meal, a fill-up of gasoline, or a mortgage on a new home.

Look for the name **Tim Kirk** on the mailboxes on the right-hand side of the staircase leading up to the apartments next to Tune-In Lounge. Imagineer Tim Kirk was the art director/concept designer for segments of the Great Movie Ride, Tower of Terror, *Indiana Jones Epic Stunt Spectacular*, and Muppet*Vision 3D.

Eddie Valliant, private investigator, advertises his service on the window above the Hollywood & Vine restaurant, to the right of Gertie and just across the pavement. Although he insists on "No Toons," if you look closely you may notice **Roger Rabbit** isn't far away.

Before you leave Echo Lake, take a quick peek at the **Cosmetic Dentistry** building, just around the bend from Hollywood & Vine restaurant and across from the Dockside Diner. There is a directory on the right-hand wall next to the door that advertises for C. Howie Pullum, DDS; Ruth Canal, DDS; and Les Payne, DDS.

The building next to Cosmetic Dentistry has a **For Rent** sign in the upper window, which isn't particularly compelling on its own, but as with all things Imagineering, it was placed there for a reason. When Walt and Roy Disney were just starting out, their initial base was in an uncle's garage until they amassed enough money to rent their own studio space. They finally found a location they could afford, right above the Holly-Vermont Realty company, whose logo you will see on the door below the For Rent sign. A nice tribute to a humble start, don't you think?

Sights and Sounds Acting and Voice Lessons, on the corner of Echo Park Drive and Sunset Plaza, has "Finished some of Hollywood's finest," but it's hard to say if that's a good thing or not. Their dubious reputation is further enhanced by the people who work there. Say the name **Ewell**

M. Pressem out loud and you'll know what I mean. **Singer B. Flatt** and the money-grubbing **Bill More**, account executive, don't inspire confidence, either.

Hollywood Hills Amphitheater

Purpose-built for Hollywood Studios' nighttime entertainment offering, the amphitheater plays to sellout crowds every night in peak seasons.

Fantasmic!

Hollywood Studios' nighttime spectacular, *Fantasmic!* showcases Mickey's struggle against the Disney villains, all with a happy ending and the chance to see many of the Disney movie characters. The riverboat ferrying the characters at the end of the show is a replica of the boat in **Steamboat Willie**. Notice who is up in the wheelhouse piloting the boat?

Imagine That!

Fantasmic! first appeared in the Disneyland park in California, and there were a few glitches to work out before its debut. Disney Legend Ron Logan remembers: "I was asked to create a spectacular for Disneyland, which had no big night-time show. With 75,000 visitors during the day, the parades weren't enough to absorb the crowds. We had water, and we had Tom Sawyer Island, so I thought, what can we put there? Walt Disney Imagineering said we couldn't change the island, so I said, 'Can we put a dock in front that blends with the island?' They agreed to that, so I said, 'What if we have speakers that come up out of the ground for the night-time show and transition back into the island during the day?' That was okay too. At the same time, we were closing the Golden Horseshoe Revue, and the show's comedian, Wally Boag, happened to be good friends with Lucille Ball. We did a party for the last show, and Lucy showed up. I was wearing a new suit because I knew I'd be meeting her, and at one point she and I were making small talk when a technician came in and said to me, 'Is it okay to test the water canon for that *Fantasmic!* show?' I went outside with him, and he said, 'Ready?' Well, he shot the cannon off and it threw water all the way to Pirates of the Caribbean! I was absolutely drenched. I said, 'I think we need to do a little work on that water cannon.' When I went back inside Lucy just looked at me and said, 'What the hell happened to you, honey?'"

And with that, it's a wrap!

Disney's Hollywood Studios Timeline

In April 1985, the Walt Disney Company announced plans to build a third gate at Orlando's Walt Disney World Resort. The $300 million park would be based on "the Hollywood that never was—and always will be." On May 1, 1989, Disney–MGM Studios welcomed its first guests, offering just five attractions, two theaters, one exhibit, a walking tour, a handful of "streetmosphere" actors, eight restaurants, and four shopping outlets.

The attractions that opened on May 1 were the **Great Movie Ride**, **Backstage Studio Tour**, **Superstar Television**, the **Monster Sound Show**, and the **Magic of Disney Animation** with the film *Back to Neverland*. Also open was the **Behind the Scenes Special Effects** walking tour, **SoundWorks** exhibit, and **Theater of the Stars** featuring *Now Playing*. Shortly after the grand opening, on August 25, the ***Indiana Jones Epic Stunt Spectacular*** held its first performance, with audience members playing bit parts in the show.

On August 24, the excitement surrounding the **Star Tours** attraction, due to open at the end of 1989, cranked up a notch as the **Ewok Village** opened at the future attraction's entrance. Then, on December 15, the ride itself, based on the massively popular Star Wars films, blasted directly into thrill-ride megahit fame.

1990: Muppets, Turtles, and Fireworks

The Broadway-style live musical *Dick Tracy Starring in Diamond Double-Cross* premiered in the Theater of the Stars on May 21, 1990, followed a day later by another new show, *Here Come the Muppets*, a stage performance with Kermit and Friends designed to generate interest in the Muppet attraction due to open the next year.

Five- to twelve-year-old boys everywhere were ecstatic when the **Teenage Mutant Ninja Turtles**, whose street show and meet-and-greet opportunities drew enormous crowds, arrived at Disney–MGM Studios. Youngsters were also the target market for the *Honey, I Shrunk the Kids* **Movie Set Adventure** (based on the 1989 movie, *Honey, I Shrunk the Kids* starring comedian Rick Moranis), which opened on December 17, 1990.

But the brightest addition in 1990 was the visually spectacular **Sorcery in the Sky** nightly fireworks finale, an awe-inspiring pyrotechnics display with the Chinese Theater in the foreground.

1991–1992: Frogs and Princesses

On February 16, 1991, less than a year after its first performance, *Dick Tracy Starring in Diamond Double-Cross* closed. It would be replaced by **Hollywood's Pretty Woman** show on September 24.

In May 1991, **Jim Henson's Muppet*Vision 3D** began serving up in-your-face laughs, both on screen and throughout the theater. The *Here Come the Muppets* show closed in early September to make way for a new attraction, but, having formally acquired the rights to use Muppet characters in the Disney parks after Muppet creator Jim Henson's death in 1990, Disney–MGM Studios unveiled the **Muppets on Location: Days of Swine & Roses** street show and meet-and-greet on September 16. Shortly after, characters from the television show *Dinosaurs* took over traveling stages originally intended for the Muppets when the **Dinosaurs Live!** parade rolled in on September 26.

Beginning on November 22, 1991, **Beauty and the Beast: Live on Stage** dazzled guests, young and old, as the characters from the movie of the same name were brought to life in the Theater of the Stars. The princess craze had begun.

Voyage of the Little Mermaid, a live musical extravaganza, started 1992 off on the right foot. Ariel and a host of puppet characters sang and danced their way through scenes from the 1989 blockbuster movie *The Little Mermaid*, while, out in the streets of Disney–MGM Studios, the year ended on another high note as the characters from cinematic smash hit *Aladdin* marched along the parade route in **Aladdin's Royal Caravan**, debuting in December.

1993–1995: Towering Achievements

Things were quiet indeed as Disney–MGM Studios ran on autopilot through 1993. In honor of television's greatest actors, the **ATAS** (Academy of Television Arts and Sciences) **Hall of Fame Plaza** was unveiled, featuring busts of beloved entertainment icons from the 1930s to the present day.

However, on the other side of the park the noise level was about to ratchet up by several decibels. Ground broke on May 28 for a massive new thrill ride, due to open in little more than a year.

Every park has a stampede attraction, and on July 22, 1994, Disney–MGM Studios opened the gates and the mad dash to the end of Sunset Boulevard began! **The Twilight Zone Tower of Terror** officially opened its doors and the enthusiastic screams have not stopped since. It would be another five years before the park welcomed a new attraction, but for now, the tower offered plenty to keep the thrill-ride fanatics happy.

In 1995, the Backlot Theater played host to **The Spirit of Pocahontas** stage show, which opened in support of the big-screen movie, *Pocahontas*. On November 22, heroes from the blockbuster movie *Toy Story* began marching down Hollywood Boulevard in the new **Toy Story parade**, replacing the lovable Aladdin and his friends. Over the years, guests had been asking for more character encounters, and Disney responded. Meeting beloved animated favorites had become an integral part of the theme park experience.

But the shining jewel in the 1995 crown had to be the premiere of the **Osborne Spectacle of Lights**, a dazzling nighttime presentation shown only during the Christmas season. Buildings along Residential Street were decorated with elaborate light displays, along with dancing vignettes, sculptures, vast archways, and seasonal slogans, all made with millions of multicolored lights.

1996–1998: The Quiet Years

Disney–MGM Studios coasted along with a few relatively minor changes from 1996 to 1998 as funds and attention were focused on creating Disney's fourth gate, **Disney's Animal Kingdom**. *The Spirit of Pocahontas* show was replaced in 1996 by **The Hunchback of Notre Dame: A Musical Adventure**, another live musical featuring characters, some in the form of puppets, from the movie *Hunchback of Notre Dame*.

After a two-year run, the *Toy Story* parade was replaced by another movie-inspired offering, the **Hercules: Zero to Hero Victory Parade** in December 1997 and, in response to the popularity of R.L. Stine's bestselling book series, Goosebumps, the **Goosebumps HorrorLand Fright Show** brought the books' scary central characters to life along New York Street in a fiendish street show young boys seemed to love.

Later that year, the Osborne Spectacle of Lights was expanded and renamed the **Spectacle of Lights with the Osborne Family Light Display**, and was by that time a huge Disney fan favorite.

Hercules and friends marched in their final parade performance in May 1998. On June 19, Disney's **Mulan parade** arrived, with brand-new characters from the feature film *Mulan*, which premiered in movie theaters on the same day.

1998–1999: Fantastic? No, *Fantasmic!*

Sorcery in the Sky was no longer showing as of 1998, and the need for a new evening show was of pressing importance. On October 15, *Fantasmic!* premiered, a character fest starring Mickey Mouse as he battled the forces of good and evil, and the show immediately drew record nighttime crowds. The 6,900-seat, purpose-built Hollywood Hills Amphitheater filled up nightly to standing-room-only crowds (to a total capacity of 9,900). *Fantasmic!* gave the park a huge boost in the form of much-needed evening entertainment.

The unusual audio-adventure **Sounds Dangerous Starring Drew Carey** replaced the original Monster Sound Show, plunging visitors into darkness while Detective Carey bungled his way through a crime scene.

A year later, on July 29, **Rock 'n' Roller Coaster Starring Aerosmith** debuted, bringing the Hollywood Studios firmly into the realm of theme park status. It was an odd fit, having nothing to do with Hollywood, the big screen, or the little screen, but it was welcomed enthusiastically nonetheless.

The park's youngest guests, most of whom would not make the new attraction's 4-foot height requirement, were not forgotten. In February 1999, television characters Doug, Skeeter, and Patti Mayonnaise from the show *Doug* delighted young guests with a new stage show, **Disney's Doug Live!**

In August, a second stage show—spun off from the beloved children's television show of the same name—**Bear in the Big Blue House: Live on Stage** worked its gentle magic, heralding a new emphasis that would permeate the parks over the coming years. Preschoolers and attractions that appealed to them were now very much on Disney's radar.

Disney–MGM Studios was a far cry from its humble beginnings. It now truly had something for everyone.

2000–2001: TV Takeover

The park remained quiet in 2000, but, in April 2001, television's über-hit *Who Wants to Be a Millionaire* spawned the theme-park equivalent in **Who Wants to Be a Millionaire—Play It!** The new attraction proved to be so addictive, at one point there were restrictions on how many times per day each guest could be a contestant. With a grand prize of a three-night Disney Cruise (with airfare!), the repeat factor was enormous. However, most hot-seat winners walked away with a pin or a hat.

On October 1, 2001, Walt Disney World also launched its **100 Years of Magic** celebration. Disney–MGM Studios honored its founder with a new attraction, **Walt Disney: One Man's Dream**, featuring exhibits, artifacts, and a lovely ten-minute film showing the highlights of the great visionary's life.

The same day, *Bear in the Big Blue House* became **Playhouse Disney: Live on Stage** (starring Bear, with his television friends from *Rolie Polie Olie*, *Stanley*, and *The Book of Pooh*). The show would have several character changes over the years; characters from *JoJo's Circus* replaced those from *Rolie Polie Olie* in March 2005, and *Mickey Mouse Clubhouse*, *Handy Manny*, and *Little Einstein* characters joined JoJo and friends in January 2008.

The *Mulan* parade ended in March 2001 and was replaced on October 1 by a more general offering, Disney **Stars and Motor Cars**, featuring favorite Disney movie characters along with classic characters, some riding in appropriately themed cars. Mr. M. Mouse and company were in attendance, and even the *Star Wars* characters got in on the action!

2003–2007: High-Octane Thrills

The following two years, 2003 through 2004, were fairly quiet, though Residential Street underwent an extensive rerouting in 2003 to make way for a Disneyland Resort Paris import called *Moteurs . . . Action! Stunt Show Spectacular*. On May 5, 2005, **Lights, Motors, Action! Extreme Stunt Show** roared into Disney–MGM Studios, adding dynamic, high-octane energy to the far left corner of the park. Real movie-making had come to life!

C.S. Lewis's classic *Chronicles of Narnia* stories were made into a feature film, *The Chronicles of Narnia: The Lion, the*

Witch, and the Wardrobe, in 2005. It would go on to win eleven Academy Awards and a place in Disney–MGM Studios. On December 9, 2005, **Journey into Narnia: Creating *The Lion, the Witch, and the Wardrobe*** opened in an empty soundstage on Mickey Avenue, a veritable winter wonderland of artifacts and costumes from the movie, storyboards, and walk-through exhibits, accessed through massive red doors resembling the famous fictional wardrobe.

Aimed at the preteen crowd, **High School Musical Pep Rally**, originally ill-placed in Magic Kingdom, found a new home as a mobile street show at Disney–MGM Studios on January 21, 2007. The East Side High Wildcats whipped the crowds into a frenzy of pep-rally cheering. The show was revamped and renamed **High School Musical 3: Senior Year–Right Here!** with less "you can be anything" preachiness, more song and dance, and a big high-school helping of audience participation.

2008: A Whole New Name

On August 9, 2007, the president of Walt Disney Parks and Resorts, Meg Crofton, announced an impending name change at the Studios, emphasizing the park's new focus on a broader range of entertainment. Then, on January 7, 2008, Disney–MGM Studios formally became **Disney's Hollywood Studios**.

In recognition of the merger between Disney and Pixar Studios, the Stars and Motor Cars parade was replaced on March 14 by the high-energy **Block Party Bash**, featuring a host of Pixar characters dancing and playing their way along the parade route, with a maximum of guest interaction.

Then, on May 30, the ambitious **Toy Story Midway Mania!** attraction debuted, placing a firm punctuation mark on the park's dedication to family entertainment, and guests of all ages were truly delighted. The Journey into Narnia walk-through exhibit was transformed into **Journey into Narnia: *Prince Caspian*** in June, and featured props from the second movie. In February 2009 **the *American Idol* Experience** debuted, bringing the popular television show to Hollywood Studios, adding even more live, hands-on appeal to the energetic Hollywood experience.

2009–2014: Show Shuffling and Final Curtains

A slow period followed the grand opening of Toy Story Midway Mania! which lasted until the big announcement of a reimagining of the Star Tours attraction. **Star Tours** closed September 8, 2010, as it received a new theme and new visuals. **Star Tours: The Adventures Continue** officially opened on May 20, 2011.

Disney-Pixar Block Party Bash had its final performance on January 1, 2011, and **Pixar Pals Countdown to Fun!** parade, which debuted on January 16, 2011, had a twenty-seven-month run, ending on April 6, 2013.

Journey into Narnia: Creating *The Lion, the Witch, and the Wardrobe* closed on January 1, 2008, and **Journey into Narnia: *Prince Caspian*** replaced it on June 27, 2008, closing on September 10, 2011, to make way for **the Legend of Captain Jack Sparrow** show, which opened on December 6, 2012, and closed on November 6, 2014.

The *American Idol* Experience opened on February 14, 2009, with its final performances on August 13, 2014, nearly five months ahead of its originally announced closing date of January 1, 2015, and **the Backlot Tour with Catastrophe Canyon** ended September 27, 2014, sparking rumors of a major expansion—or two!—coming to Hollywood Studios.

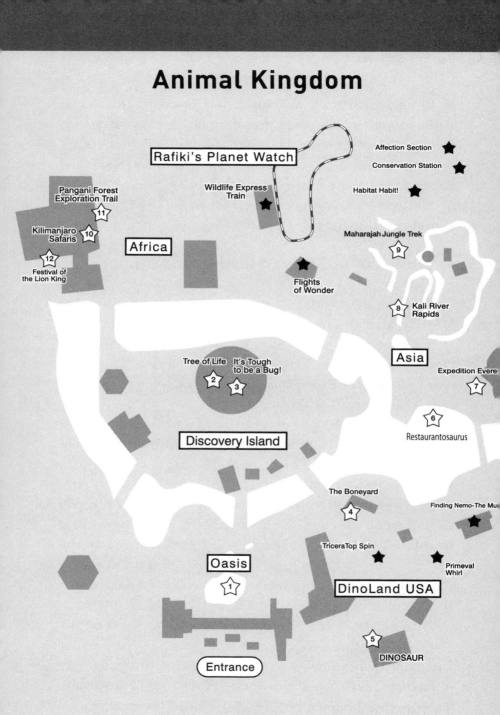

Animal Kingdom

Rafiki's Planet Watch

Affection Section ★

Conservation Station ★

Wildlife Express Train ★

Habitat Habit! ★

Pangani Forest Exploration Trail ⑪

Kilimanjaro Safaris ⑩

Festival of the Lion King ⑫

Africa

Maharajah Jungle Trek ⑨

Flights of Wonder ★

Kali River Rapids ⑧

Tree of Life ② It's Tough to be a Bug! ③

Asia

Expedition Everest ⑦

Restaurantosaurus ⑥

Discovery Island

The Boneyard ④

Finding Nemo–The Mus ★

TriceraTop Spin ★

Primeval Whirl ★

Oasis ①

DinoLand USA

DINOSAUR ⑤

Entrance

1. **Oasis:** At the front of the Oasis you'll find the park's dedication plaque engraved in a large rock at the center of the landscaping under a light fixture, with opening-day comments from Michael Eisner.

2. **Tree of Life:** There is hidden magic in the Tree of Life that goes beyond the variety of animals. The tree's texture also represents a variety of barks, including cedar, oak, banyan, magnolia, and pine.

3. **It's Tough to Be a Bug:** The first time you hear a child crying during the show, you're actually hearing a recording, designed to turn your attention to the audience, just as the bugs have.

4. **The Boneyard:** On the right-hand side of the Boneyard is a rock formation with rib bones showing through the strata. Go ahead and push on each one. You've found the musical xylobone.

5. **DINOSAUR:** The dark layer running parallel to the queue, about halfway up the wall, represents the K-T boundary, the scientific demarcation point between the age of dinosaurs and the age of mammals.

6. **Restaurantosaurus:** It's not a ride, but it certainly is an attraction. Restaurantosaurus is filled with fabulous little gems that make DinoLand feel like a real working environment.

7. **Expedition Everest:** If you are near Expedition Everest after dark, notice the lighting. It is a nod toward the way the sun hits the mountain at twilight in Nepal.

8. **Kali River Rapids:** The canoe paddles with names and comments on them hanging on the walls as you walk through the Kali Rapids Expeditions office are scrawled with the signatures of the attraction's Imagineers and designers.

9. **Maharajah Jungle Trek:** The photographs in the hallway outside the bat enclosure are of real caves in Asia, and the man in one of the pictures with his back to the camera is none other than Animal Kingdom's lead Imagineer, Joe Rohde.

10. **Kilimanjaro Safaris:** Invisible barriers have been set up in each environment along the safari's route. Mud wallows, deep ruts, watering holes, waterfalls, stone outcroppings, fallen trees, and even heavy foliage create natural boundaries that help define each enclosure.

11. **Pangani Forest Exploration Trail:** The Visitor Information board just after you exit the trail features a letter to the Harambe Research Team with a list of eight organizations you can join to become a genuine member of the research team once you get home.

12. *Festival of the Lion King:* Join Simba, Nala, Rafiki, and the rest of the gang in this once-in-a-lifetime theater experience!

Chapter 4

Disney's Animal Kingdom

Jambo! Welcome to Disney's Animal Kingdom, where the message is clear: Observe and appreciate the intrinsic value of nature. The beauty of the living world surrounds you, but beware—there is an unmistakable element of danger around every corner, too!

In direct opposition to every other theme park in Orlando, the slower you take your day at Animal Kingdom the more you will see, so a second important word to remember while touring here is *meander*. A deliberate, appreciative wander will reward you with visual delights around every corner, tucked into every landscape, and over every bridge. The animals are, literally, everywhere. Some are real, some are not—but all hold unending fascination for those who take the time to look.

Imagine That!

From blue-sky thinking to the final product, Ron Logan shares what makes Disney Imagineers special: "You have to go through different filters before anything can be created. You've been through every challenge, every 'disease' there could be. It's that attention to detail that sets Disney apart. The Disney Difference is that you work harder."

Entrance

Animal Kingdom's first secret becomes obvious before you even enter the park. See that tall, thin tree that rises up to the left of the parking lot? It's a cellular phone tower, a necessary encroachment that looks out of place on its own but blends in (at least, a little bit) when made to look like part of the landscaping. You can see it best after you pass through the toll gate, before you actually reach the parking lot.

To avoid wandering the parking lot in a frustrated daze at the end of the day, guests are encouraged to remember their parking section by its animal designation: Giraffe, Butterfly, Dinosaur, Peacock, or Unicorn. The Unicorn section is a throwback to the original plans for the park, which included a **Beastly Kingdom** section, filled with mythical animals. Dragons and unicorns were intended to figure heavily, and you'll see them scattered around the park, on signposts, park logos, and even on the ticket booths.

The dragon's head above the ticketing center on the right is an obvious reference to the never-built Beastly Kingdom, but there are two more **mythical beasts** in the carved panels as well. See if you can find them, then check out Solution 4 in Appendix: Solutions to Hints at the back of the book.

Imagine That!

When considering the entrance for Animal Kingdom, the Imagineers came up with several creative options. Imagineer Joe Rohde states, "We know that we want to bring people into this park in some way that is different than the way they have gotten into the other parks, which are about human stories and are very architectural environments." Some of the early concepts, as described by Rohde, involved an ark entrance (too controversial), animals marching into the park (too many backsides pointing at guests!), a woodsy art nouveau village with little cottages (too hippie), or a huge, cavernous grotto (too much cement). The grotto idea became the launching point, finally evolving into a lush oasis with small cavern-like coves.

The ground under your feet holds a secret, too, and it starts just after you exit the tram. Those long, wavy red and green patterns embedded in the pavement form a **giant mural** of sorts. If you follow one of the flowing imprints, you may get the idea it's the branch of a tree, and you'd be right. The green pattern represents the Tree of Life, captured in cement. Can't quite make it out? Google Earth it when you return home! Or, look at an old park map.

The Oasis

Disney's Animal Kingdom follows a subtle evolution, beginning in the lush surroundings of the Oasis. There are no rides here and very little evidence of human impact on the environment, animal tracks crisscross the pavement, and there is a distinct and deliberate lack of human footprints. This is the world prior to the dawn of humankind, a peaceful haven before civilization sets in.

Be patient as you wander through the area. Animals move at their own paces, and the Oasis encourages you to follow suit. You may have noticed you are walking up a slight incline as you wind your way through the environment. The gentle hill you are climbing is intentional, prompting you to slow your steps and immerse yourself in nature's splendor.

April 22, 1998, was Earth Day, the perfect day to open a park honoring the world of animals and nature, Disney's Animal Kingdom. At the front of the Oasis you'll find the park's **dedication plaque** engraved in a large rock at the center of the landscaping under a light fixture, with opening-day comments from Michael Eisner.

A major theme in Animal Kingdom is conservation, with an emphasis on environmental awareness, not only in the park but also on a global level. One testament to Disney's dedication to recycling can be found right under you when you take a seat. All the benches in Disney's Animal Kingdom are made of **recycled milk jugs**.

The Oasis offers an easy opportunity to see one of the **invisible barrier** methods used to keep the animals safely in their habitat. Standing as close to an enclosure as possible, look for the thin metal spokes sticking up in bunches of three. They blend seamlessly with the environment if you are not looking for them, but they are effective barriers that do not harm the animals in any way while maintaining a natural look inside their living environment.

Imagine That!

Even with a long list of shows and attractions under their own belts, Imagineers, designers, and casting executives still admire their coworkers' accomplishments. Ron Rodriguez shares his sentiments about Animal Kingdom's lead designer: "Joe Rohde's got chops. If he was a musician, we'd say he's got chops. The Adventurers Club at the former Downtown Disney Pleasure Island was Joe's creation, too. Most of the artifacts came from Joe's house."

Discovery Island

The Tree of Life is an awesome achievement, standing 145 feet tall, carved with 325 reptiles, mammals, and birds, all designed to take your breath away the instant you walk from the Oasis into Discovery Island. The bridge between the two areas is wide in recognition of the fact most guests will stop dead in their tracks when they see it. While the view from here is astounding, one to be savored slowly as your eye travels across its 160-foot expanse for the full impact, it is even more incredible up-close, and you will get close enough to touch its roots in just a moment. Have cameras at the ready; your journey takes you underground shortly.

There is hidden magic in the Tree of Life that goes beyond the variety of animals. The tree's texture also represents a **variety of barks**, including cedar, oak, banyan, magnolia, and pine.

Along with the **reticulated giraffe**, which was carved into the tree in honor of the first animals to make their home at Disney's Animal Kingdom, two other animals were included for a special reason. The **manatee** and the **armadillo** have a place on the tree as the representatives of Florida's wildlife.

See if you can find them, and if you're stumped take a look at Solution 5 in Appendix: Solutions to Hints.

Fascinating Fact

When Animal Kingdom opened, many guests wondered if there were any animals in the park. Sightings were "disappointing," so the Imagineers had to find ways to coax reclusive residents out into the open to enhance the guest's experience. Using the "you can lead a horse to water" theory, they created landscaping that held a certain appeal to the animals—a watering hole, a feeding opportunity, or a cool spot on a hot day—while maintaining a natural look within the environment. Many of the stumps, trees, rocks, water features, or reed beds you see may actually be a feeding station or an air conditioner, attractive features for the wildlife resulting in better viewing opportunities for guests.

It's Tough to Be a Bug!

The last animal you see before you walk through the turnstiles is the chimpanzee, and in this case, a very special chimpanzee. As the Tree of Life was being carved, Jane Goodall, the world's foremost authority on chimpanzees, was invited for a viewing. As the story goes, she asked where the chimpanzee was located and, because chimps were somehow overlooked, a carving of the chimp Jane named **David Greybeard**, the first chimpanzee observed making a tool in the wild (and thus redefining the popular understanding of what it means to be human), now holds a place of honor on the Tree of Life. And he'll hold you, too, so climb up on his lap for a photo. Then, look to your left where you will find a small plaque on the wall telling Jane's story. As an interesting aside, David Greybeard is the only named animal on the entire tree.

Once the show starts, a brilliant piece of Disney Imagineering literally pops right up. The animatronic version of **Hopper** in *It's Tough to Be a Bug!* is 8 feet tall and is one of the most complex animatronics ever made. Hopper also plays a not-so-obvious role. His sudden, angry appearance signals the beginning of the end for many children viewing the show. When Hopper arrives, cue the crying! In fact, Disney itself cues the crying. That **first cry** you hear is actually a recording, designed to turn your attention to the audience, just as the bugs have.

Take time to explore the tree's carvings after you exit the show, making a full circuit around the roots. As you wander, see if you can find the **scorpion**. It is actually an Imagineer signature of sorts. Zsolt Hormay, chief sculptor and senior production designer of the Tree of Life, included the scorpion and a cuddly **koala bear** in the design, at the request of his young son and daughter. Can't find them? See Solution 6 in Appendix A: Solutions to Hints.

Imagine That!

The Tree of Life concept presented a problem for Imagineers, who originally intended it to have a restaurant and a children's play area inside. Concept drawings included a geodesic dome serving as the canopy portion of the tree, requiring a sturdy support system. As often happens, the challenges led to solutions that changed the entire direction of the idea. Imagineer Joe Rohde recalled, "Very late in the process, one of the engineers came in and said, 'Now that we have designed the steel and the branches to hold up that geodesic dome, those branches would hold up anything. We don't need the geodesic dome because the tree is so strong that we could just hold up the branches themselves.' So we rapidly reconceptualized the tree to become the tree you see today."

Before you leave Discovery Island for adventures beyond, take note of a bit of hidden magic that's right in front of your eyes, though you may not have noticed it. It's clear that each of the buildings has a nature motif, but did you notice that each of them has a specific theme? Island Mercantile's theme involves **migrating animals**, the animals at Adventurers Outpost all **live in or around water**, those at Creature Comforts are **patterned animals**, and Disney Outfitters celebrates **animals that live in herds**. It's obvious now that you know, isn't it?

Two of the nearby restaurants also got into the act, with the rooms at Pizzafari and pavilions at Flame Tree Barbecue having a **predator/prey** element to them. You're surrounded by one species bent on making a meal of another, and you symbolically become part of the act as you devour lunch or dinner.

While you're looking for predator and prey combinations at Flame Tree Barbecue, notice the **rhinoceroses** that appear to be charging from under the restaurant's roofline. They have birds on their heads, and while rhinos don't eat birds and birds don't eat rhinos, they do have a symbiotic relationship that still works within the theme. The end result of a rhino's meal ultimately provides a meal for the birds.

DinoLand U.S.A.

Pass under the Olden Gate Bridge (groan!) and the world of dinosaurs opens up in front of you. You're not actually visiting during the time of the great beasts though. Instead, you're working with a group of scientists and student paleontologists who have unearthed a treasure-trove of fossils.

But there is a distinct feeling that the two groups may not be completely in harmony. For the students, it's all about fun. The scientists, however, are on a serious mission, and the divide in their territory (and in their thinking) is symbolized by the changes in the pavement. The area's red pavement is the realm of the scientists; the dirt-like pavement is the paleontologists' stomping ground and the location of their dig sites.

The Boneyard

One of the first areas you come across after you pass under the Olden Gate Bridge is the Boneyard Dig Site, a great place to let children loose while adults take a much-needed break. But even the most tired tourists will find some of the Boneyard's hidden secrets entertaining enough to get up off their crates and take a look (or a listen).

Before you enter the Boneyard, notice the wrapped **stegosaurus shoulder blade**. It is a real casting, but it's in the shape of Animal Kingdom before Asia was added. The orientation mark N for north and the arrow show which side is up. While it is less obvious since Disney introduced the current style of park map, you can still compare the sign to your map and get a vague idea of the layout.

The **bulletin board** across from the entry to the Boneyard further enhances the difference between the prankster students and their long-suffering professors. But another conflict is revealed here, too. Read the **Notice section** printed in the Dino Institute's newsletter, at the bottom left corner of the right-hand panel. Security has issued a plea for help in reporting those pesky relatives of Chester and Hester, who have been hanging around the dig site and are certainly up to no good.

Just under the notice is a second plea in **A Word from Dr. Dunn**, which details one of the pranks the students have played on their professors.

Off to the right near the Jeep in the Boneyard, you'll see a rock formation with rib bones showing through the strata. Go ahead and push on each one. You've found the musical **xylobone**.

Go around the corner to the left of the xylobone, if you're eager to follow in the tracks of some of Earth's biggest reptiles. Step on the **footprints** embedded in the ground and you may hear a growl, a trumpet, or a roar erupt from the caves behind you.

You wouldn't expect to see a tiny stairway leading up to a **miniature door carved into the rock** while you're exploring for dinosaur bones, but there it is, in the rock formation to the left of the dinosaur tracks, which begs the question: What's back there? Go ahead . . . open the door. I dare you.

Next, take the stairway up to the second level after you pass the picnic table. There is a small area near the entry to the red, blue, and yellow tube slides, where the students base themselves during digs. Check out some of their **paraphernalia** and the funny comments on the blackboard where their work schedules are posted.

Dinosaur fossils aren't the only treasure in DinoLand. Tacked to the upper right-hand corner of the bulletin board just across the pathway from the dig site is a **hand-drawn map of DinoLand** as it existed when the park first opened.

Imagine That!

Ron Rodriguez recalls the creative process during his time with the company: "Disney afforded the freedom to be innovative. You could do anything; you could experiment. It wasn't a 'known.' It was, 'Let's try it and see what happens!'"

Restaurantosaurus

It's not a ride, but it certainly is an attraction. Restaurantosaurus is filled with fabulous little gems that make DinoLand feel like a real working environment, but it does have at least one foot in reality. You can't miss the big silver **Airstream Travel Trailer** sitting right outside the restaurant which, in real life, belonged to the grandmother of Imagineer Todd Beeson.

Restaurantosaurus was the **old institute** before their smart new building was built. The Great Room was the institute's exhibit hall, and the Bunk Room was the former dining room.

If you look at the roof of the restaurant before you enter, you'll see that the student paleontologists bunking down in the attic of the Restaurantosaurus are definitely out to cause trouble. They have been shooting makeshift plunger arrows at the **water tower** from a lawn chair on the roof of the restaurant.

The **dinosaur painting** to the left of the four dinosaur heads on the left-hand wall in the counter service area was created by none other than Joe Rohde, lead Imagineer for Disney's Animal Kingdom. Look closely at the bottom right-hand corner just under the fern leaf and you'll see his signature.

Head around the corner to the opposite side of the dino-head trophy wall and you'll find a genuine treasure of Disney memorabilia. A set of **four pen-and-ink drawings** from the 1940s Disney film *Fantasia*, in which the drawing's scenes were set to Igor Stravinsky's *The Rite of Spring*, depicts the creation of the planet and the rise and fall of the dinosaurs.

Somehow, Chester and Hester have infiltrated the students' hangout. Although the original picture of them holding hands is on a high shelf in Dinosaur Treasures, you'll also see an **American Gothic Revisited**—style poster made from that picture in the main dining room to the left of the cash registers.

The Hip Joint, just off the Bunk Room, is the place to hang out after a long day of dig, dig, digging. Scattered all over the walls are references to some of the students and their favorite jukebox music has a familiar sound but with a slight twist. Listen closely and you'll hear songs you may recognize, all updated with a dinosaur theme. The radio in the Hip Joint is tuned to WDINO, and if you listen closely you'll hear their tagline, "**Can you dig it?**"

Exit Restaurantosaurus by the side door across from the DINOSAUR attraction and pause a moment to look at the first window on your left. A careless student has left a **dinosaur bone** on the window ledge. Why hasn't it been moved (or stolen)? Go ahead, try to pick it up. It seems to have fossilized to the ledge.

DINOSAUR

It's pretty hard to miss a 40-foot-long, 20-foot-high meat-eating Tyrant Lizard King, so it is unlikely you will overlook the *Tyrannosaurus rex* charging out of the foliage on the right-hand side of the pathway leading up to the DINOSAUR attraction. She is an exact replica of Sue, the largest, most complete, best-preserved *T. rex* ever found.

Walking through the Dino Institute as you queue for DINOSAUR, you enter the rotunda area where it feels as if you have not only gone back in time, but also underground. Strata along the walls give a clue to how far you have traveled into the earth. That dark layer running beside you, about halfway up the wall, represents the **K-T boundary**, the scientific demarcation point between the age of dinosaurs and the age of mammals.

Imagine That!

Describing what Walt Disney Imagineering does, Eddie Sotto, Senior Vice President of Concept Design with WDI, beautifully captures the department's intensity and excitement when he says, "WDI is the perfect storm of imagination, technology, and design that transforms impossible dreams into timeless realities. To me, the thrill ride formula is pretty simple, it's: Fear minus death equals fun."

If you aren't too frightened about your impending trip back in time, pay attention to the name of the scientist who is about to send you on your search-and-recovery mission. His name is **Dr. Grant Seeker**. (Another groan!)

Because DINOSAUR is a popular ride drawing long lines throughout the day, you should have plenty of time to look at the scenery as you wind your way down to your Time Rover. While standing on the stairway just above the loading area, take a look at the pipes running down toward the track. The **chemical formula** painted across the red pipe is the chemical makeup of ketchup, the yellow pipe displays the formula for mustard, and the white pipe is, of course, the formula for mayonnaise.

After you board your Time Rover, notice the indication **Vortex Capacitor Sector WDI CTX AK 98** on the right-hand wall. There are several references here, including Walt Disney Imagineering (WDI); Countdown to Extinction (CTX), which was the name of the attraction when it first opened; and the name and opening year of the park (AK 98).

As you make the first right turn heading toward your journey back in time, notice the **dry erase board** to your left. Newly hired Cast Members sign the board after they have finished their Traditions training.

Your knees may be shaking when you exit the attraction, but you can recover from your trip in relative peace and quiet if you take the shady trail between DINOSAUR and Chester and Hester's Dino-Rama, just to the left of the attraction's entrance. Pause for a moment to regain your balance and listen closely for the sounds of dinosaurs in the brush. Then, as you walk toward the shop at the end of the trail, notice how the pavement changes. Remember the **demarcation line** between the scientist's area and the student's archaeological site? It's even more obvious along the trail in this area.

Chester & Hester's Dino-Rama

Chester and Hester Diggs, the eccentric proprietors of Chester & Hester's Dino-Rama, are definitely the local yokels, with a sense of style that is seriously kitschy! But they do know a great opportunity when they see one. They turned their little plot of land into Dino-Rama, a garish roadside carnival, after their dog unearthed a bone that turned out to be a dinosaur fossil. The Diggs saw dollar signs, refusing to sell their land when the Dino Institute caught wind of the geological treasure-trove beneath their feet, instead adding to their empire with Dino-Rama.

Every good roadside attraction has its gift shop, and you'll enter Dino-Rama's just past the shady trail you took from DINOSAUR. Chester & Hester's Dinosaur Treasures recalls the tacky roadside souvenir shops dotted across America, and some would say, still prevalent in the Kissimmee/Lake Buena Vista area today. There is an awful lot to look at here, but pay particular attention to the **photograph** on a shelf on the left side in the center of the store. It shows Chester and Hester in all their glory, and it also holds a bit of a secret. There's something a bit odd about them, isn't there? Can you figure out what it is? Give it a shot, then look at Solution 7 in Appendix: Solutions to Hints.

While you're browsing in Chester and Hester's Dinosaur Treasures, notice how the shop was formerly their **car-servicing station**. The side doors near the gas pump are garage bay doors, and if you look at the floor you'll see some of it was formerly road surface, some was the garage floor, and some is hard-packed mud.

Most of the **phone numbers** scribbled on the walls near the pay telephone weren't put there by naughty tourists. They were added as part of the atmosphere, with the inactive prefix 555. Read them and you'll discover some are competing companies for Chester and Hester's former service station.

Hester isn't fooling around. Look at the **Posted** sign on the wall just below the ceiling, to the left of the pay telephone. Trespassers won't be prosecuted, they'll be fossilized!

Fascinating Fact

Dinosaur Sue takes her name from the amateur fossil hunter Susan Hendrickson, who discovered the bones in South Dakota in 1990. Sue is a unique specimen in that she was found with a complete breast-bone. She is also one of only two *T. rex* fossils discovered with an arm intact. In 1998 Disney's Animal Kingdom received some of Sue's bones, and scientists from the Chicago Field Museum (which made the successful bid at auction for the bones) moved into a fossil preparation lab on public display in DinoLand to begin the cleaning process. The bones were then shipped back to Chicago and Sue now stands proudly (and fiercely) in the Chicago Field Museum's main lobby. Another interesting fact, Sue's skull alone took 3,500 hours to clean!

The sign on the roof of Dinosaur Treasures indicates Chester and Hester are having a **Going Out of Existence Sale**, but the real gems here are the names on the drawing of the planet. The bottom one reads **Gondwanaland**, and it isn't a made-up word. Gondwanaland existed 570 million years ago and was one of two supercontinents that fused to form Pangaea before splitting apart again during the Jurassic era. The name on the land mass above Gondwanaland is **Euramerica**, also known as Laurussia, which was the second "half" of Pangaea.

There are **three large billboards** at the back of Dino-Rama, to the right of Primeval Whirl. One of them advertises the attractions you're experiencing in DinoLand, but also references the *Tyrannosaurus rex* "Sue." Sue's articulated bones can be seen on the right-hand side of the pathway leading to the DINOSAUR attraction, but it is also a tribute to Dino-Rama's original function. Before Chester and Hester moved in, this part of the park featured the real bones of the *T. rex* dubbed Sue, and guests could watch as her bones were being cleaned.

On the same billboard, just over the right shoulder of the cartoon dinosaur, you'll see **498**, which is another reference to the opening date of Disney's Animal Kingdom.

Take a look at the various **gas pumps** around Dino-Rama. The prices set the area's time frame at 1953–1957.

Primeval Whirl

You can't miss Dino-Rama's main attraction, just outside Dinosaur Treasures. Primeval Whirl packs a real punch, and it's Chester and Hester's less costly time-travel answer to DINOSAUR. But it also pays homage to another Walt Disney World attraction. See those three **dinosaurs hitching a ride**? Do they remind you of another Disney classic? If you thought of Haunted Mansion's hitchhiking ghosts, you'd be right!

Chester and Hester either have a bad case of Science Institute envy or they'll do anything to make a buck. Either way, Primeval Whirl is their version of a journey back in time. Without the funding the institute has, the creative couple has resorted to using **common household items** to create their time machine.

Before you exit Dino-Rama and head past the giant orange "concreteasaurus" toward Asia, pay attention to **Highway U.S. 498**, which runs around the carnival, creating a subsection of sorts within DinoLand. Exit toward the Boneyard play area, taking note of the hedges that spell out the name of the area, boarded in **license plates** from different states across the nation. Highway U.S. 498 is also a reference to the opening date of Disney's Animal Kingdom—April 1998.

There is no themed greeting in DinoLand, but there are a few **themed farewells**. When you leave the area, be sure to say, "Rock On!" or "Dig ya later!" to one of the Cast Members.

Asia

Welcome to Anandapur (pronounced "Uh-NON-duh-pour"), the "place of delight"! As its name implies, enchantment awaits at every turn, capturing the essence of Asia in minute detail. The pavement beneath your feet shows an evolution that not only includes the imprint of human feet, but also a great feat in the evolution of transportation. People are not just walking in Asia; they're also riding bicycles, a popular mode of transportation in these parts. However, at the base of the mountains you will only see human prints and hoof prints. You are now too high up for bicycles, and pack animals are the transportation of choice.

The **foliage imprints** in the mud pathway also change as the symbolic elevation changes, going from palm fronds in front of Trekkers Inn, to long pine needles on the pathway outside the Yeti Museum, to pin oak leaves in the courtyard of Serka Zong Bazaar.

As you think about the name of the attraction, an interesting detail may occur to you right away. Although you are on an expedition to climb Mount Everest, the legend here is really about the **Forbidden Mountain**. The train ride will take you to a base camp on the Forbidden Mountain, where preparations for the ascent will take place. However, there is something standing in the way, and it's a big, angry something!

Imagine That!

The Forbidden Mountain could well be called Mystery Mountain. Because it was essential the designers could see the mountains as they were being built (to preserve scale, forced perspective, etc.), traditional scaffolding could not be used. Instead, the Imagineers came up with the creative idea of toothpick scaffolding. Once in place, over 2,000 toothpicks (steel beams) stuck straight out of the mountain, with flat bases for the builders and artists to stand on as they worked, leaving a near-complete view of the mountain range as it went up. Finally, each toothpick was cut off, leaving no trace of the scaffolding. If an architect in the future were to look at the design without seeing the schematic, they would be hard-pressed to figure out how Everest was built. Another interesting tidbit: In the past, using clay models, it would have taken three years to complete the design for Everest. With today's computer technology, it only took eighteen months.

You may have noticed there is a lot of **paint** throughout Serka Zong, on the buildings, statues, signs, and other artwork. Red is considered a color of protection, a magic spell of sorts that keeps evil spirits at bay. **White paint** represents the underworld, **black** is the "spirit maker," and the totems ward off evil spirits. The village's inhabitants are paying close attention now that the Yeti has been angered.

Fascinating Fact

Everything in Serka Zong has a symbolic meaning, including the three stripes on shrines, which represent three spirit worlds. These worlds have various regional names, including Svarga, the upper world where gods live and humans reside until their reincarnation; Prithvi, the middle world of people and all known things; and Patala, the underworld, home to demons.

The long **red and black stripes** cascading down the exterior of Serka Zong Bazaar indicate that the family who own the shop and live above it are rich, have old money, and have ties to the monastery.

What is that bright red building to the right of Serka Zong Bazaar? It's a **gompa**, a Buddhist religious-learning fortress. Gompas may be nunneries, homes to monks, or retreat centers. It's no wonder the inhabitants here have covered the building in protective red paint.

Why is there **no snow on Everest**? Because the sun can be fierce at the summit and the winds are so powerful they often blow the snow away, exposing sheer rock.

What's with the waterfall tumbling down the Forbidden Mountain? It represents **melting glaciers** pouring down the mountainside, setting the seasonal time frame between May and September. Sir Edmund Hillary and his Sherpa guide Tenzing Norgay summited Mount Everest in late May, making the time frame appropriate to their historic climb. Also in honor of their climb, the **Hillary Step**—a treacherous 39-foot wall of ice along the final push to the summit—is represented in the view of Everest from Serka Zong.

If you are near Expedition Everest after dark, notice the lighting. It is a nod toward the way the **sun hits the mountain at twilight** in Nepal.

The voice you hear between musical interludes at the unused train station entry to the left of the temple is **Joe Rohde's**.

Expedition Everest—Legend of the Forbidden Mountain

Your journey up the mountain and into the lair of the Yeti begins in the village of Serka Zong, progressing through Norbu and Bob's booking office for Himalayan Escapes, past the Yeti Mandir, into Tashi's Trek and Tongba Shop, and finally making your way through Professor Pema Dorje's Yeti Museum, which was once an old tea warehouse, before you begin your trip into the unknown.

Begin in Norbu and Bob's, where the name of their tour company, **Himalayan Escapes**, has the double meaning of an escape *to* the Himalayas and an escape *from* them.

In a slight break from the story of a Himalayan village, Norbu and Bob have a **Disney Wildlife Conservation Fund** sticker lying on their desk.

Sir Edmund Hillary and his Sherpa guide Tenzing Norgay, the first two people to summit Mount Everest, are honored with the inclusion of the book *Tenzing Norgay and the Sherpas of Everest*, which sits on a shelf in Norbu and Bob's office. It was written by Tenzing's grandson, Tashi Tenzing, whose first name happens to be the same as a certain trek and tongba shop here in Anandapur. Sir Edmund Hillary and His Holiness the Dalai Lama wrote the book's forward.

Within the context of Anandapur's story, the **nondescript rock** next to the large shrine in the center of the courtyard after you exit Norbu and Bob's was sacred to the locals, and the village grew up around it. It now has offering cups on top of it, symbolizing its revered status.

The **coins all over the courtyard** weren't added by the Imagineers. Instead, they have been tossed there by tourists heading up the mountain. Since they don't look out of place they're allowed to stay. The coins are collected periodically and donated to the Disney Worldwide Conservation Fund, so feel free to add a few to the collection.

The trek part of Tashi's Trek and Tongba Shop is obvious. But what does *tongba* mean? It's a millet-based alcoholic drink popular in Nepal, with a sour, yeasty flavor. It is traditionally served hot, making it a good warmer on a cold Himalayan night. Tashi's has everything trekkers could need to make their journey more comfortable, but if it is uncomfortable, at least the beer will take the edge off. Look for a tongba mug on the table in Tashi's, and several for sale on the shelves, complete with specialized drinking straws.

Fascinating Fact

Tongba is ale, but not as we know it. Instead of popping the cap off of a beer bottle, the drink is typically served in a heavy wood or bamboo mug called a tongba, from which it takes its name. It is made from a thick base of fermented millet into which hot water is poured, and the resulting cloudy liquid is consumed through a special straw that filters out the millet. More hot water is added and the process is repeated until no more flavor—or alcohol—can be extracted.

The large cabinet you come to just after you make the first turn in the queue inside the Yeti Museum holds an important piece of Mount Everest research material. The faded blue book behind the propane stove recalls the speech **"Observations on the Rocks and Glaciers of Mount Everest"** given by N.E. Odell to the Royal Geographical Society on May 18, 1925. The presentation covered Everest's geography in great detail, including maps and photographs taken during a five-month expedition during which Odell, a geologist, served as the climbing party's oxygen officer.

You will find two more references honoring Tenzing Norgay and Sir Edmund Hillary in the Yeti Museum. One is a **picture of Norgay,** in the second large cabinet you come to as you're walking through the queue. The shorter case to its left holds a copy of the July 13, 1953, edition of **LIFE magazine** featuring the explorers' summiting of Mount Everest.

Displayed in cases and on shelves are **statues of the Yeti**, with his hand raised. These statues mimic Hindu and Tibetan god and goddess statues, and in some instances, the Yeti holds the Forbidden Mountain range in his hand, his other hand raised in a warning to turn back. The statues themselves symbolize his status as a spiritual being.

Fascinating Fact

The sense of realism is immense due to the Imagineers' attention to detail and the fact that there are more than 2,000 authentic items throughout the attraction that were handcrafted in Asia. Many every-day items were purchased in Nepal to ensure authenticity. Even the nails holding up pictures on the wall were purchased from locals. They look like the real deal because they are the real deal.

Norbu and Bob are on a mission to **convince tourists the Yeti doesn't exist**. Notice the sign on the wall to your right just before you exit the Yeti Museum. It's obvious they don't want you to cancel your upcoming trip.

While **Professor Pema Dorje, PhD**, curator of the Yeti Museum, isn't a real person, the picture you see of him on the left just after you enter the museum is none other than Expedition Everest's Senior Production Designer, Daniel Jue.

Read the letter Professor Dorje has received, just below his picture. It is from **Russell A. Mittermeier, PhD**, who is a real person. He was the president of Conservation International from 1989 until September 2014, and he is considered one of the most important wildlife conservationists in the world. In 1999, Mittermeier was named one of *TIME* magazine's Heroes for the Planet.

Take a moment to notice the document hanging to the left of the praying monkey statue in the Anandapur Mountaineering Association shop, the first building you enter if you are using FastPass+. Renowned mountaineer, author, poet, and conqueror of Everest, Pat Ament's humorous book *10 Keys to Climb Everest* is apparently required reading before making the trek up the mountain. Curiously enough, so is *Walt Disney Imagineering*, written by (who else?) the Disney Imagineers. You'll see a copy of the book on a shelf under a crouching wooden tiger.

While you are waiting to board, notice the **boiler at the back of the train**. It isn't practical to have a full load of water onboard this particular steam train, so Imagineers employed a little magic. Watch closely, and you'll see the steam actually comes up through the train from the tracks below shortly before it sets in motion. Where does the steam originate? It starts in the boiler you see to the right of the boarding area. You'll pass it as you begin your journey.

The train doesn't chug out big **puffs of soot**, so to make it look realistic, soot has been painted on various surfaces in the train station, adding to the atmosphere of a place that's meant to be old and well-used.

As you exit the attraction, dazed but unharmed, your newfound appreciation for the sanctity of the mountain may inspire you to send up your own prayer of thanks for a safe return. And the place to do it would be the **prayer wall** you see off to the left as you are walking up the stairs to the main pathway. Common in Tibetan culture, carved mani (prayer) stones are often piled up near mountain passes, temples, lakes, and other outdoor areas, providing a sacred place for the faithful to pray.

But the biggest secret of Everest is this: The Yeti *isn't* feared as an evil, destructive creature. He is honored, in every way you have just observed and in real life among the Himalayan people, as the spiritual **Protector of the Mountain**. Sure, he's going to chase you away as soon as you reach the summit, causing your train to careen wildly down the mountain. But hey, he's only doing his job. You dared to enter the realm of the Yeti!

In reality, Everest is rarely the tallest mountain you see from any location and because it is usually viewed from a distance, closer mountains appear to be larger. With that in mind, Imagineers created a **peekaboo moment** (a quick glimpse of something interesting from other areas in the park) with the telescope you see next to the shrine as you leave the Everest area heading farther into Asia. Look through the telescope and you will see it is focused on the mountain to the right of the highest peak. That's Everest. The highest mountain you see is the Forbidden Mountain, and its placement in front of Everest giving the illusion of height is another form of forced perspective.

The shrine to the right of the telescope isn't a random design, either. The **outline of the shrine** represents the shape of the mountain range across the lake. Bend down a bit and the shrine will align with the mountains. The **placement of the Yeti** in the lakeside shrine mimics his placement inside the attraction.

The **Yeti Palace Hotel** hasn't been built yet (as the sign painted on the wall indicates, it will be Opening Next Season), but it's on its way in response to the growing number of tourists visiting Anandapur.

What's with the **long walk from Anandapur to the Siamang temple**? You're making the trek out of the Himalayas, aren't you? That's a long way to go!

The owners of the Yak & Yeti Restaurant aren't as prone to superstition as the villagers are, so you'll see no protective symbols here.

But if you're dining with them today, notice the free-form **painting around light switches** and other functional elements, a decorative touch used in homes and buildings in Nepal.

Kali River Rapids

Kali, the Hindu god who lends her name to the river in Animal Kingdom's Asia, is the goddess of time and of the transformation that comes with death. She is the ferocious incarnation of the Divine Mother and is believed to create the fear of death in the ignorant while removing that fear in those who seek knowledge. With that little tidbit in mind, are you ready for a ride down her river?

The queue delights the eye with thousands of authentic artifacts, but pay attention to the sounds as well. At various points you will be able to hear **loggers** cutting trees in the distance, an indication of what's to come on your journey down the rapids.

The **Trekking Guide of Anandapur Township** sign, just off the main path between the Siamang temple and the outdoor dining area of the Yak & Yeti Restaurant, lists a certain **Seven Summits Mt. Trekking**, recalling the Seven Summits Expeditions window on Main Street, U.S.A., honoring Frank Wells, president of Walt Disney Company from 1984 until 1994, who was an avid mountaineer.

Another feature of the Trekking Guide is that all the locations listed in blue are places you can actually visit in Anandapur, while those listed in red are fictitious. **Chakranadi Chicken Shop** falls somewhere in between; it was a real dining spot in Anandapur, but it closed in 2006 to make way for the Yak & Yeti Restaurant.

The building on stilts on the left side of the pathway leading to the queue for Kali River Rapids is someone's home, and they're not the wealthiest people in the village. Notice the **floral curtains** at the windows. One of them is a shirt.

The beautiful paintings on the ceiling of the temple just after you enter the covered portion of the queue are based on a vast body of Buddhist literature called **Jatakas**. Similar in style to the old European fairy tales, the Jatakas are stories of the Buddha's lives, which offer moral guidance to his followers.

A sign posted on the wall just before Mr. Panika's Shop gives tourists an idea of what they can expect from the nearby hotel. Take note of the warning, **"mattress and toilet paper just a little extra."**

As you walk through Mr. Panika's Shop, notice how he has employed his best English to attract more tourists. He didn't get it exactly right, but his signs reading **"looking looking is free please you kom in our store"** and **"spesial prices for tourists"** show he's making an effort.

Mr. Panika will do just about anything to make a sale. The sign above his desk reads, **Antiks Made to Order**, and it doesn't mean "antics," it means "antiques." Want to take home a special souvenir of your visit to Anandapur? Mr. Panika will assemble something quickly and you can tell your friends it's ancient. They'll never know the difference.

Kali Rapids Expeditions keeps a close eye on what their raft excursions are up to, and the Manaslu Slammer raft hints at a problem. The chalkboard listing each of the **expedition rafts and their current disposition** indicates the Slammer was due back yesterday. But don't worry about your rafting trip. What could go wrong?

Look for the **canoe paddles** with names and comments on them hanging on the walls as you walk through the Kali Rapids Expeditions office. Some of them are the signatures of the attraction's Imagineers and designers. Cast Members who work at Kali River Rapids are also allowed to sign a paddle when they leave so that they are always a part of the attraction.

Those pesky loggers are at it again. Stop for a moment and listen to the radio in the office, just before you board your boat. The announcer warns there is **illegal logging in the area**, giving you some idea of what you will encounter as your raft makes its way through the jungle. Unfortunately, the owner of Kali Rapids Expeditions isn't in the office, and has missed the warnings. It looks like your tour will proceed in spite of the danger.

Once you are settled in your raft, look at the rockwork on the left side of the river as you approach the top of the first lift hill. If you have a sharp eye, you'll see the **face of a tiger** carved into one of the rocks. In the planning stages, the attraction was called Tiger River Rapids and the face carved here is a nod toward its former name.

When your raft careens over the edge, you're not going over a waterfall, though that seems like the obvious circumstance. Instead, your drop indicates **the land has been decimated** and is now giving way beneath you.

Imagine That!

Realistic environments are a key element in the parks, but one of the main goals is to bring guests fully into the story in ways beyond the visual. Immersing guests in evocative sights, sounds, textures, and scents is of primary importance, as Imagineer Joe Rohde explains: "It's got to feel like nature, not just look like nature. If you feel the naturalness, then you're going to feel the threat all the more, which is, of course, the threat to harvest out the value of nature and turn it from intrinsic value to monetary value. Therein lies the conflict that is at the source of almost every story at Animal Kingdom."

Maharajah Jungle Trek

After your harrowing journey down Kali River Rapids, you're probably ready for a more relaxing adventure along Maharajah Jungle Trek, which winds its way through the Royal Anandapur Forest.

Why have newspapers been stuffed into the ceiling of the building at the entry into Maharajah Jungle Trek? They're an **inexpensive form of insulation**.

Nature has taken over what was once the Royal Hunting Palace of the Maharajahs, but the villagers make use of the abandoned rooms, too. Notice the **movie camera** suspended from the ceiling in the fruit bat enclosure. This is a community room, where films are shown and special events take place. If you look at the **calendar** on the wall just after you exit the enclosure you'll see what's on the agenda for this month.

When you leave the bat enclosure, look to your right and you'll see a series of interesting pictures in the hallway. The **photographs** are of real caves in Asia that were inhabited by bats, though they were not the bats you see here. Even better, the man in one of the pictures with his back to the camera is none other than Animal Kingdom's lead Imagineer, Joe Rohde.

Murals along the jungle trek tell the story of the maharajahs who once lived here. The first prince you see on the left was a hunter who felt it was his right to control the natural world, while the prince on the right cared only for the material world. As the balance between man and nature broke down, the third prince attempted to regain order, and the fourth prince, surrounded by birds, allowed nature to take over as he left the palace and found peace among the animals.

As you walk along the pathway, notice details such as the **black and white floor tiles** of the former ballroom, **support columns** that no longer hold up a roof, and **walls** that once separated rooms in the hunting palace. They are partially obscured by foliage, telling a story of nature's retaliation over man's indifference.

As you browse the shops before leaving Asia, notice the picture of the **Royal Couple of Anandapur**. Every shop will have one, not only to honor Their Highnesses, but also to show how wealthy the shop owner is. The bigger the picture is, the wealthier the owner.

Another feature you will come across as you make your way along the path is a re-creation of something commonly seen in small villages around Asia. The **drinking fountain** surrounded by various pots and pans mimics the tradition of villagers placing their vessels at local water taps, catching the small stream of water that leaks from the spigot. When one pot is full, a passerby will swap it for an empty one so that everyone gets their share of water and nothing is wasted. How friendly!

Four **bas relief panels** at the end of the trek, to your right shortly after you cross the bridge, highlight the story of man against nature, and the breakdown of balance and order.

Africa

You have finally reached Africa, the cradle of civilization. Hoof-prints dot the pathways, leading off into the lush underbrush. Human influence is evident, but there is a sense of cooperation between people and animals, a feeling of balance, with neither overpowering the other. Enter the village of Harambe and you'll find a bustling settlement full of music, wildlife, and some fascinating hidden gems. Of all the lands in Walt Disney World, Africa is the one that most closely resembles the real thing. Every building you see here is an exact replica of an existing building in Africa, right down to the cracks and crevices.

Imagine That!

Imagineer Eric Jacobson, senior vice president of Creative at WDI, describes the meticulous process of moving a concept from rough idea through to the "cracks and crevices." "We like to say—and we follow this extensively—it all starts with a story. In everything we do, we have a story that we're following so that the entire team knows what the goal is and what story we're telling. Then, all that layering from the initial outline to the script to the physical building to all the detail supports the story line that we developed in the beginning. We may modify it or massage it along the way, but basically we all follow that one path. Just by doing the detail and those extra things, it brings the story to life in a way that people really appreciate."

The time period is post-British rule, with evidence of the occupation (such as the iconic British **mailbox** near the restrooms across from Tusker House) and of East Africa's subsequent freedom.

Take note of the directional sign next to Tamu Tamu Refreshments as you approach Harambe, and in various other locations around the village. The date you see on the sign's base, **1961**, signifies the year the Republic of Kenya began its road to Independence, when Jomo Kenyatta won the presidency of the Kenya African National Union. That date ties Disney's fictional Harambe to Kenya's real town of Harambee. But another important event took place in 1961, too. Tanganyika (later called Tanzania) in East Africa became fully independent of British rule on November 1, 1961. Because Animal Kingdom's Africa is a blending of many African nations, that political change is also relevant, and is honored through the motto **Uhuru**, the Swahili word for "freedom," which you will find in various locations throughout Harambe.

As you wander around Africa, take note of the **signs directed at foreign visitors**. Some of them employ proper English, a reflection of the area's former British rule. Some, however, have a little bit of trouble with the language, and while the message is sincere, the results can be humorous.

Even Dawa Bar has a hidden meaning. In Swahili, *dawa* literally translates to "medicine," but in connection with a bar it means something along the lines of **"party medicine,"** inviting guests to have a drink.

Stop for some party medicine at Dawa Bar and take a look at the **framed photograph** to the right of the Specialty Cocktails menu. The man in the center wearing an elaborate costume is Joe Rohde, lead Imagineer for Disney's Animal Kingdom, and the child seated on his knee is his son, whose face was removed and substituted with the face of an adult. The signature next to the child indicates his name was also changed, and now he's known as **Eric the Dwarf**. The picture was taken at Joe Rohde's home during a wrap party for Animal Kingdom.

You may not notice anything particularly intriguing about the Hoteli Burudika, just past Dawa Bar as you walk toward Kilimanjaro Safaris, but take a look anyway. See that notice posted on the wall with the peculiar word **Jorodi** on it? Say it slowly. It's a hidden Imagineer signature, and by now you can probably figure out whose! Some of the other signs also refer to Imagineers who helped design Animal Kingdom.

The address for Jorodi Masks and Beads is **Ushaufu Way**. *Ushaufu* has several meanings in Swahili, including "frivolity," "something misleading," "something disappointing," and "vanity." However, it does have another meaning: Translated as "pendant," it is an appropriate reference to Joe Rohde's signature earrings.

Fascinating Fact

Thatch is a near-perfect roofing material. It's fire resistant, highly insulating, and it lasts up to forty years. Thatched roofs in Animal Kingdom's Africa section, with the exception of those near Harambe Theater, were made by thatchers from Zululand in South Africa.

Festival of the Lion King

In 2014, Harambe Port's **Theater District** was added to Africa to accommodate the *Festival of the Lion King* show, which moved when Camp Minnie-Mickey closed to make way for an *Avatar*-themed land. The story of Harambe Port revolves around a former fort, which has been repurposed as a theater for traveling entertainment.

But the theater isn't the only business in town. **Bars on the windows** above the theater's exit reveal that this part of the fort has been turned into a jail. Next to the theater's exit is the **Ubongo Center of Learning**, while several other businesses, including an artist, a hairdresser, a silversmith, a traditional healer, and a local offering computer classes have taken over the former **Customs and Clearance center** and the building formerly occupied by **His Majesty's Imperial Protectorate Mail Service**.

Imagine That!

Many of Disney's special effects, such as the dancing ghosts in Magic Kingdom's Haunted Mansion, are fairly high-tech, but some are decidedly low-tech. The short wall just outside of Harambe Theater looks as if it has been there for fifty years, but the aged effect was created by an artist flinging handfuls of concrete against the wall to give it texture, then painting on algae and other details.

The area is still rural, as evidenced by the warning painted on the wall to the left of Hoteli Burudika as you cross into the Theater District. It reads, "Hakuna ruhusa ya kufunga mifugo mbele ya ukuta huu," which translates to, "**No permission to install livestock in front of this wall.**" Take your cows elsewhere, but heed the same warning posted on a column in front of the restrooms next to Tamu Tamu Refreshments.

Just as the visitors to Hoteli Burudika while away the hours above the Dawa Bar, those who work in the theater district enjoy their break time on the roof of the Customs and Clearance Center. There is even a **satellite dish** on the roof, supplying television service to the area.

Flyers on telephone poles advertising the theater's show read, **"Maonyesho ya mfalme simba. Utendaji mizuri. Inafunguliwa siku zote. Kiribu nu Harambee Beach."** They translate to, "Performances of Lion King. Good performance. Opening all day. Synergy Beach closed now." In Swahili, "harambee" means "let us all pull together," or "synergy."

Take time to read the signs posted along the queue as you make your way toward the festival. Immediately after entering the queue you'll see a humorous reference to **rascally baboons**, and a plaque indicating you are in an **Official Harambe Heritage Site**, with the date 22-4-98. Although it states Harambe Fort was built in 1498 rather than 1998, by now you know the date is a reference to the opening day of Disney's Animal Kingdom, written in the day-month-year format used in Europe and Africa.

The signs in the Customs and Clearance archway reading Usiegamia Kuta are a reference to the appeal Cast Members are always making as guests wait in long lines. They translate to, **"Please do not recline on the wall."**

Just before you enter the theater, notice the sign to the extreme left of the doors. It advertises the **Mpira Tyre Company**. In Swahili, *mpira* means "tire" (spelled "tyre" in Africa), "rubber," and "ball," making it a fitting name for the company.

Kilimanjaro Safaris

There is no mistaking Animal Kingdom's message of conservation as your safari takes you to the African savannah, and the power of being directly immersed in the animals' natural habitat brings that message home in a real and immediate way. Although the environment is closely controlled in some ways, this is one of the few attractions in Walt Disney World where almost anything truly can happen. You never know where the savannah's residents might be at any given time and you never know what you might see. Every journey is different, and in this place the animals dictate where the magic will be found.

Kilimanjaro Safaris' story line changed in 2012, and instead of highlighting the dangers of poaching it became the story of **Africa's challenges today**. Baby elephant Little Red is gone, the poachers have been captured, and now you're on a photo safari to appreciate Africa's diverse wildlife. While park warden Wilson Matua still mentions poaching as you make your way toward your vehicle, once onboard the story focuses on the animals' loss of habitat.

Going on safari in Africa has its challenges, and your challenge today is to get a **giraffe selfie**. When you reach the Serengeti grasslands, see if each person in your group can snap a picture of his or her face with a giraffe in the background. The results are even funnier if you try it with your camera instead of your smartphone.

Imagine That!

Kilimanjaro Safaris presented a unique problem for the Imagineers, who recognized the unpredictability of the show environment. Designer Joe Rohde describes how they dealt with the challenge: "Unlike a scene in a ride where you can direct people to 'look over here,' we knew two things: one, you can look wherever you please, and number two, we will never know where the focal object is going to be, which is an animal. The animal could be anywhere and you can look anywhere. So when we did our storyboards, we drew a line on the ride track estimating the average speed of the vehicle, made a dot every thirty seconds, and we drew 180-degree storyboards that we would hold up in front of our faces and go, 'Okay, that's at second number 700, we're here, seeing something like this.' The wildebeests might all be over here, they might all be here, but they're going to be in this scene. We'd pick up the next one, bend it around our head and, all right, this is the next scene. So we could get some sense of what is this going to be like to progress through this environment because, of course, back then we couldn't do a digital ride-through. No such thing existed."

During your tour notice the clever way **invisible barriers** have been set up in each environment. Mud wallows, deep ruts, watering holes, waterfalls, stone outcroppings, fallen trees, and even heavy foliage create natural boundaries that help define each enclosure. Less obvious barriers, such as deep moats and stepped underwater edges, help keep the animals in their own habitats.

Fascinating Fact

For the animals' safety, many of them must return to a shelter for the night. How do they know when to return? As you now know, each species responds to a specific sound. Out on the savannah, zebras return when they hear a cowbell, giraffes return to the sound of a sports whistle, most of the hoofed animals respond to a horn, and the Thomson's gazelles have the most unusual signal—they come running when they hear a goose call.

Animals are not the only ones making use of the savannah. Just after your tour passes Flamingo Island, look at the **outcroppings** on either side of your Jeep. The local tribe has added an artistic touch to the rocks.

For the enjoyment of passengers, your driver will tune in to music on the Jeep's radio, which plays an uplifting, inspiring tune. It is a composition called "Hapa Duniani," incorporating a modified version of **Baba Yetu** (the Lord's Prayer) in Swahili, as sung by the Voices of Celebration. Beautiful!

There is more to explore, this time on foot. Your next adventure waits just around the bend, to the left of the exit for Kilimanjaro Safaris, in the form of a walking path that was originally known as Gorilla Falls Exploration Trail. The name changed shortly after the park opened, but the respite from Africa's hustle and bustle remains.

Pangani Forest Exploration Trail

Pangani, a small town in Africa in the Republic of Tanzania along the Indian Ocean coastline near the border with Kenya, was once an active center of trade but is now a peaceful retreat, as it is here in Animal Kingdom. When Animal Kingdom opened, Cast Members along the exploration trail played the role of the **students working in the area**. Now they are just called attendants.

Just before you enter Pangani Forest Exploration Trail you'll see a small trolley on the right-hand side, which holds crates, equipment, and tools. One of the crates, marked **ZU2298 Radio**, references the park's opening date, but also holds another little secret. Stand next to it and listen for a special transmission.

At the beginning of the trail you'll pass through an **archway** that is, literally, a piece of Imagineer handcrafting. The simple mud structure became a work of art when the designers applied their bare hands to the job, leaving their prints on the arch as they applied its rough surface. Even Executive Designer Joe Rohde and Concept Architect Tom Sze left their imprints on the walls, re-creating a timeless building technique while adding their own silent signature to the work.

They aren't a secret and they aren't really hidden, but most guests don't notice the **Herpetology Field Notes** along Pangani Forest Exploration Trail. Take a look; they make for interesting reading.

Fascinating Fact

If you're inspired by what you're experiencing in Animal Kingdom and you want to support animal conservation, here's a hidden gem just for you: The Visitor Information board just after you exit the trail features a letter to the Harambe Research Team with a list of eight organizations Disney supports. Take a picture or jot them down, and become a genuine member of the research team once you get home.

Keep walking along the path and you will come across a scientific research station with a small animal whose name is ridiculously comical, especially for the twelve-and-under crowd. The **naked mole rat**, pink and hairless, isn't pretty, but it's a fascinating creature just the same. They communicate through a vast repertoire of whistles and chirps, their sole mission in life is to serve their queen, and they use their buck teeth—which can move independently of each other—to dig tunnels and, to the delight of young viewers, subterranean toilets. But the most interesting thing about the naked mole rat is that it is the only cold-blooded mammal on Earth.

On the shelf next to Dr. K. Kulunda's desk in the research station you'll see a large book with the title *Animal Kingdom*. While it is about animals of the world, it's an obvious reference to both the name and the theme of the park.

Rafiki's Planet Watch

Arriving at Rafiki's Planet Watch, the focus turns to the synergy of the natural world, eventually including humans in that equation. As you walk toward the main building, notice how the **animal engravings** in the pavement demonstrate this sense of working together. At first, each animal is independent from the others; then as they progress further into the area, they come together as a cooperative community. Finally, the large circular engraving shows (literally) how all creatures are inextricably entwined.

Kilimanjaro Safaris and Pangani Forest Exploration Trail allowed the animals to tell their own tale, but here at Rafiki's Planet Watch, the focus turns to what humans can do to keep the scales balanced. Notice the enormous **mural at Conservation Station**. Each animal looks directly at guests, signaling its quiet expectation of human respect and assistance in the natural world's survival.

As you depart the train at the Harambe Train Station after your visit, head out the right-hand exit and notice the words **Vyombo Vya Stesheni** painted on the building just beyond the train station. They translate to "station instruments," roughly meaning the building contains "things necessary for the station."

Return to Africa and backtrack to the pathway leading out of the Port of Harambe. You will eventually come across a unique set of lights designed to look like ladybugs. They are the only **ladybug lamps** in the whole park, and they serve as a landmark for Cast Members. First Aid is also located here, and even the most novice CM is fully aware of exactly where to find it, using the ladybug lights as the landmark.

As you wind your way out of the park at the end of a long, rewarding day, let your pace slow to a meander and pause to enjoy the small details that add an extra element of depth to the stories unfolding around you.

Imagineer Joe Rohde summed it up best when he said, "Just as we hope to bring joy and inspiration to our guests, we hope that they take that inspiration out into the world. See it every day in the living world around them and act upon that inspiration. That is the heart of Animal Kingdom."

Disney's Animal Kingdom Timeline

Forty years after Walt Disney's first theme park in Anaheim, California, opened, the Walt Disney Company announced their intention to build what would arguably be their most unique and challenging park yet. It would take another three years of development, but finally, on April 22, 1998, Disney's Animal Kingdom swung the gates wide and welcomed its first guests.

Attractions open that day were **the Boneyard** dinosaur dig area, **Countdown to Extinction**, **Cretaceous Trail** walking paths, **Discovery River Boats**, *Festival of the Lion King*, **Flights of Wonder** exotic bird show, **Gorilla Exploration Trail**, *Journey into Jungle Book* stage show, **Kilimanjaro Safaris**, *Pocahontas and Her Forest Friends*, **Rafiki's Planet Watch**, and **Wildlife Express Train**. There were six distinct areas on opening day:

the Oasis, Safari Village, Africa, DinoLand U.S.A., Camp Minnie-Mickey, and Conservation Station. A seventh area, Asia, was due to open within a year, with the mythical Beastly Kingdom also on the drawing board.

Beastly Kingdom would cover the "animals of myth and legend" portion of the park, a land of fire-breathing dragons and gentle unicorns; of *Fantasia*'s fauns, centaurs, and dancing hippos; the world of fantasy and fairy tale brought to life. It was an incredible concept, but it has yet to be realized.

1998–1999: First Expansion

By the end of 1998, Gorilla Exploration Trail would be renamed **Pangani Forest Exploration Trail**; the Discovery River Boats would close, reopening two months later as **Discovery River Taxis**; and, a month later, Discovery River Taxis would make its final run—sort of. It would reopen in March 1999 as **Radio Disney River Cruise**, a jaunty music and banter-filled boat ride to nowhere (that also closed down before the end of the year, another formula that just didn't work). The March of the ARTimals also paraded for the final time in 1999.

However, there was something new to enjoy, and it was substantial. The new section of Asia opened on April 22, 1999, with the soak-you-to-your-skin river-rafting experience, **Kali River Rapids**, and the peaceful **Maharajah Jungle Trek** walking trail. Kali originally went by the conceptual title Tiger Rapids Run and was intended to showcase animals from Asia as guests floated past in circular rafts. But these things have a way of changing, and Kali River Rapids ultimately became a whitewater saturation-fest loosely wrapped around a mild lesson about the dangers of logging.

2000–2001: Time for a Parade

Animal Kingdom sailed along happily for two more years before adding any new attractions. The beautifully artistic **Mickey's Jammin' Jungle Parade** then made its first run on October 1, 2001 (as part of the Walt Disney World 100 Years of Magic celebration), with stylized animal puppets, stilt walkers, and Disney characters riding safari vehicles. The puppets were worn by humans and were designed by Disney's *The Lion King* Broadway show puppet creators, Michael Curry Design.

There was more on the horizon, though, as Disney was aware there still wasn't enough here to keep eager fans happy and to make it more than a half-day experience in many guests' minds. The first part of it arrived in DinoLand in November 2001, and it finally gave preschoolers a ride tailored just for them. **TriceraTop Spin** was another variation on the Magic Carpets of Aladdin in Magic Kingdom (which were themselves a spinoff of the popular Dumbo ride), but they added a tried-and-true favorite, with baby triceratops ride vehicles instead of flying carpets or big-eared elephants.

2002: Dino-drama

The full development of this new area came in April 2002. **Chester and Hester's Dino-Rama** "roadside carnival" in DinoLand was certainly big all right. At least, the towering yellow brontosaurus framing the entrance was big!

As well as TriceraTop Spin, Dino-Rama consisted of a handful of paid-for carnival games, tacky (intentionally, said Disney) gift shops, and the area's saving grace, **Primeval Whirl**. Though it looked like a cheap (but again, intentionally tacky) "wild mouse" coaster with a cartoonish prehistoric theme, it was actually a dynamic, spinning coaster that packed a gut-wrenching wallop!

Many fans felt the area was the theme park equivalent of "throwing them a bone," no better than the seasonal fairs that spring up all over small-town America. But they still waited for an hour just to ride Primeval Whirl.

2003–2005: A Lucky Strike

Even that wasn't enough to keep guests coming back in droves, as the area was intended to do, since most guests still considered Animal Kingdom a half-day park. But Disney's response was slow. When it did come, in April 2005, it was in the form of a green, cart-toting, free-roaming, self-contained Audio-Animatronic baby brontosaurus with personality plus! Lucky the Dinosaur was a first in Disney's animatronic world. He could walk on two legs, pulling a cart behind him; he could grab objects in his mouth; he had a degree of vocal expression; and he could fully interact with his "handler" in a most convincing way. However, Lucky's stay at Animal Kingdom was short. By the end of July 2005, he had moved on to Hong Kong Disneyland.

Cries for a new land—ideally, Beastly Kingdom from the park's conceptual stage—grew louder. Although Animal Kingdom had begun to increase in popularity, it lacked the kind of draw that kept guests coming back again and again. But a new day was about to dawn in Animal Kingdom. The Yeti was about to arrive.

2006: Enter the Yeti

On April 7, 2006, **Expedition Everest—Legend of the Forbidden Mountain** careened into Asia with a Himalayan train ride on the fast track toward the mountain's protector, the fearsome Yeti. The coaster's precarious journey put riders face-to-face with the angry beast before making a breakneck escape down the Forbidden Mountain.

Walt Disney Imagineering had a new megahit on its hands and had fulfilled, at least to some degree, the park's original intent to include mythical creatures in the animal lineup. Attendance soared.

2007: A Musical Note

Things were going along swimmingly at Animal Kingdom, and on January 24, 2007, a new attraction officially debuted at Theater in the Wild, replacing *Tarzan Rocks*, which closed in January 2006. **Finding Nemo: The Musical** offered a charming human-puppet show featuring Nemo, Merlin, Dory, Crush, and their friends in an artistic pageant the whole family could enjoy.

Because the blockbuster movie *Finding Nemo* did not have any songs, adapting it into a musical was left to husband-and-wife team Robert Lopez, co-creator of *Avenue Q*, a Tony Award–winning Broadway hit, and Kristen Anderson-Lopez, co-creator of a cappella musical *Along the Way*, who wrote fourteen original songs for the new show.

Actors dressed in costumes similar to their character handled larger-than-life puppets, but they were fully visible to the audience. While Disney had employed this technique in Epcot's parade Tapestry of Nations and Mickey's Jammin' Jungle Parade, it was unique to an onstage, in-park musical. *Finding Nemo: The Musical* would also mark the first time Disney Creative Entertainment, a division of Walt Disney Imagineering that was created in 2001, produced a major musical show for a Walt Disney World park.

2008: Ten Years After

On April 22, 2008, Disney's Animal Kingdom celebrated its tenth anniversary with a special rededication ceremony featuring renowned primatologist Dr. Jane Goodall, who was there at the beginning of this "new species of theme park" and was happy to mark the park's milestone birthday with her own signature chimpanzee vocalization!

2009–2014: Goodbye Campers, Hello Aliens!

The land that was once earmarked for Beastly Kingdom but became an area of meet-and-greet trails underwent a major overhaul when **Camp Minnie-Mickey** closed January 6, 2014, to make way for the new *Avatar* land due to open in 2017. *Festival of the Lion King* went on hiatus when Camp Minnie-Mickey closed, and the building was moved, lock, stock, and barrel, to the Africa section of the park. It reopened on June 1, 2014.

Mickey's Jammin' Jungle Parade ended May 31, 2014, leaving Animal Kingdom with no afternoon parade but with the tantalizing prospect of all-new entertainment in the form of a **Rivers of Light** show on the park's waterway, and spectacular night-time entertainment on the Tree of Life and throughout Discovery Island.

An all-encompassing experience is at the heart of each of the Walt Disney World theme parks. You are meant to participate, becoming part of the story rather than acting as a passive observer. Let *The Hidden Magic of Walt Disney World, 2nd Edition* inspire you to seek out the finer points and allow yourself to be totally immersed in the heart of the magic.

Appendix

Solutions to Hints

Magic Kingdom

Solution 1: Find the rooster on the roof to the right of the entry door to Liberty Tree Tavern in Liberty Square. The moose is on the roof of the tower directly behind the archway to the right of Gaston's Tavern in Fantasyland; the elf-like man is on the roof to the left of the arched entryway with the sign for Pinocchio Village Haus on it; and the crocodile is behind the tower to the left of the main entry for Peter Pan's Flight, on a roofline between Peter Pan and *Mickey's PhilharMagic*.

Solution 2: The cats in Carousel of Progress can be found on a tuffet in Jimmy's room in the turn-of-the-century scene; by Grandpa's rocking chair in the 1920s scene; as a white cat book-end in the television room and a black cat printed on an orange candy bag on the dresser in Patricia's room in the 1940s scene; and snuggled up in a gift box on top of a small stack of presents near Grandma in the Christmas scene.

Epcot

Solution 3: The brown one next to the European trappers shop is the traditional totem pole. The fancier, flashier totem pole is definitely a Disney creation.

Disney's Animal Kingdom

Solution 4: Additional mythical beasts in the carvings above the ticket centers are a griffin and a winged horse. You will see the griffin to the left of each of the central heads. The winged horse is in the panels on the far left side of each building.

Solution 5: Find the manatee to the left of the waterfall near the second lamppost after you enter the queue. Find the tiny armadillo to the right of the baboon, just above the crocodile. Having trouble locating it? Look for the big eagle and keep scanning to the right.

Solution 6: Find the scorpion on the back of the tree between the hippo and the owl. Find the koala bear on the front of the tree, tucked behind the eagle's wings.

Solution 7: While no one is sure if Chester and Hester are married, if they are brother and sister, or if they are cousins, one thing is definite: That picture is a split image and the characters Chester and Hester are played by the same person.

Acknowledgments

I would like to thank Imagineers Joe Rohde, Eric Jacobson, Ron Logan, Ronald Rodriguez, Eddie Soto, Michael Roddy, Jason Grandt, Dave Minichiello, Pam Fisher, Melissa Jeselnick, Mark Hervat, Chrissie Allen, Sue Bryan, and Jason (from an impromptu meeting!); consultants Cindy White, Kal David, and Margaret Kerry; and Darwin Bravo and Samad Benzari for generously sharing their stories. I would also like to thank the Walt Disney World Cast Members for their unfailing dedication to providing a magical experience to all their guests.

Thank you to Brendan O'Neill and Shannon Smith at Adams Media.

And a very special thank-you to Gene Columbus, not only for sharing his time and his stories but also for the wonderful mentor and inspiration he has been to the next generation of entertainment industry professionals.

Index

Author Bio

Susan Veness is a travel writer, researcher, and itinerary planner specializing in Florida, Disney, and the theme parks. A former online travel agent, she became principal research assistant for the U.K.'s bestselling Brit's Guide travel series in 2002. She is the author of *The Hidden Magic of Walt Disney World Trivia*, and, along with her husband, Simon, she has coauthored four books: *The Hidden Magic of Walt Disney World Planner, Brit Guide to Orlando and Walt Disney World, Brit Guide to Disneyland Paris*, and *Silver Surfers' Colour Guide to Travel and Holidays*. She also writes for a wide variety of newspapers, magazines, and other media. Susan has been visiting Walt Disney World since it opened in 1971, and with a home just minutes from the Mouse, she continues to tour the parks on a regular basis.